PLAYING WITH PURPOSE

WRITING LIVES
Ethnographic Narratives

Series Editors:
Arthur P. Bochner & Carolyn Ellis
University of South Florida

Writing Lives: Ethnographic Narratives publishes narrative representations of qualitative research projects. The series editors seek manuscripts that blur the boundaries between humanities and social sciences. We encourage novel and evocative forms of expressing concrete lived experience, including autoethnographic, literary, poetic, artistic, visual, performative, critical, multivoiced, conversational, and co-constructed representations. We are interested in ethnographic narratives that depict local stories; employ literary modes of scene setting, dialogue, character development, and unfolding action; and include the author's critical reflections on the research and writing process, such as research ethics, alternative modes of inquiry and representation, reflexivity, and evocative storytelling. Proposals and manuscripts should be directed to abochner@cas.usf.edu

Volumes in this series:

PLAYING WITH PURPOSE

Adventures in Performative Social Science

Mary M. Gergen and Kenneth J. Gergen

Walnut Creek, California

Left Coast Press, Inc. is committed to preserving ancient forests and natural resources. We elected to print this title on 30% post consumer recycled paper, processed chlorine free. As a result, for this printing, we have saved:

3 Trees (40' tall and 6-8" diameter)
1 Million BTUs of Total Energy
264 Pounds of Greenhouse Gases
1,189 Gallons of Wastewater
76 Pounds of Solid Waste

Left Coast Press, Inc. made this paper choice because our printer, Thomson-Shore, Inc., is a member of Green Press Initiative, a nonprofit program dedicated to supporting authors, publishers, and suppliers in their efforts to reduce their use of fiber obtained from endangered forests.

For more information, visit www.greenpressinitiative.org

Environmental impact estimates were made using the Environmental Defense Paper Calculator. For more information visit: www.papercalculator.org.

LEFT COAST PRESS, INC.
1630 North Main Street, #400
Walnut Creek, CA 94596
www.LCoastPress.com

ISBN 978-1-59874-545-0 hardback
ISBN 978-1-59874-546-7 paperback
ISBN 978-1-59874-547-4 institutional eBook
ISBN 978-1-61132-580-5 consumer eBook

Library of Congress Cataloging-in-Publication Data:

Gergen, Mary M.
  Playing with purpose : adventures in performative social science/Mary M. Gergen and Kenneth J. Gergen.
    p. cm—(Writing lives)
Includes bibliographical references.
ISBN 978-1-59874-545-0 (hardcover : alk. paper) — ISBN 978-1-59874-546-7 (pbk. : alk. paper) — ISBN 978-1-59874-547-4 (institutional ebook) — ISBN 978-1-61132-580-5 (consumer ebook)
1. Social psychology. 2. Social sciences—Research. 3. Performance. I. Gergen, Kenneth J. II. Title.
  HM1033.G473 2012
  302—dc23
                    2011052657

Printed in the United States of America

∞™ The paper used in this publication meets the minimum requirements of American National Standard for Information Sciences—Permanence of Paper for Printed Library Materials, ANSI/NISO Z39.48–1992.

Contents

Acknowledgments

This volume contains selections from the following previously published pieces.

Gergen, M. 2010. Haiku Written in Honor of the 50th Class Reunion. In *Celebrating Poets over 70*, eds. M. Vespry and E. Ryan. Hamilton, Ontario: The McMaster Centre for Gerontological Studies and Tower Poetry Society.

Gergen, K. J. 2009. *Relational Being: Beyond Self and Community*. New York: Oxford University Press.

Gergen, M. and K. Jones. 2008. Editorial: A Conversation about Performative Social Science. *Forum: Qualitative Social Research* 9 (electronic journal).

Gergen, M. 2000. Woman as Spectacle. In *Postmodern Psychologies, Societal Practice and Political Life*, eds. L. Holzman and J. Morss, 93–99. New York: Routledge.

Gergen, M. 1997. Skipping Stone: Circles in the Pond. In *Toward a New Psychology of Gender: A Reader*, eds. M. Gergen and S. N. Davis, 605–611. New York: Routledge.

Gergen, K. J. and M. Gergen. 1994. Let's Pretend: A Duography. In *Life and Story: Autobiographies for a Narrative Psychology*, ed. D. J. Lee, 61–86. New York: Praeger.

Gergen, M. 1992. Life Stories: Pieces of a Dream. In *Storied Lives*, eds. G. Rosenwald and R. Ochberg, 127–144. New Haven: Yale University Press.

Gergen, M. 1990. From Mod Masculinity to Post-Mod Macho: A Feminist Re-Play. *The Humanist Psychologist* 18: 95–104. Revised for *Psychology and Postmodernism*, ed. S. Kvale. London: Sage 1992.

SECTION I

TOWARD A PERFORMATIVE SOCIAL SCIENCE

"Performative social science indeed!" This mixture of surprise and alienation often greets us when we talk about our work. The remark informs us that we are embarked on foolish nonsense, suspicious and possibly corrosive, not really science at all. How shall we respond; how can we explain our seemingly superfluous deviations? We might begin, simply, by offering a definition. We are exploring the potentials of a *performative* orientation to inquiry. We call it "performative" for three major reasons. First, we wish to call attention to the way in which our work in the sciences—as in the arts— is performed *for others*. Ultimately, we are attempting to communicate with an audience. With this consciousness of performance, we begin to consider such questions as "Who is the audience?" "What audiences are excluded?" "What responses do we hope to achieve?" and "What skills are needed in the performance?" What is to be gained, we ask, if we compare our forms of performance in the social sciences with the communicative activities across the range of the arts?

Second, in using the term performative, we draw from philosopher J. L. Austin's *How To Do Things with Words*. Here he calls attention to the way words function as actions within relationships. To ask a friend "How are you today?" is not simply a question about health or well-being; it can also serve as an act of friendship. The words accomplish something in the relationship. What then do we accomplish in the human sciences in the way we write or speak? What sorts of relationships are we creating or sustaining, to what forms of life are we contributing, and why and for whom are they valuable? For us, these are very important questions.

The third reason for favoring the word "performative" is because it expands our scope and sensitivities as social scientists. Our scientific tradition invites us to view scientific research as a refinement of the natural act of observing and reporting. As we are told, the ideal scientist suspends his or her biases in order to see the world for what it is and to report on these observations in an objective way. In contrast, the concept of performative inquiry calls attention to the significance of aesthetic skills in observing and reporting. There is nothing in the act of observing itself that will transform the "booming, buzzing confusion" into an aesthetically pleasing order, nor will observation yield a report that will *just naturally* stimulate excitement, intrigue, or fascination. We need special skills of observing and writing, skills that are so often those of the artistic performer.

To be sure, all social science inquiry is minimally performative. That is, when we present our work to others we are "on stage." But the performative dimension goes virtually unnoticed. How long has it taken, for example, to realize how PowerPoint presentations undermine the speaker's active relationship with the audience, transforming him or her into a ghostlike voice in the dark, echoing a text on a brightened screen? In placing the emphasis on the performative dimension, we hope to open new paths and potentials for doing research and communicating our work to others. You might look at the later chapters of this book as a series of "case studies" in the exercise of a performative consciousness.

Yet, can these words satisfy the defenders of tradition? Probably not. Nor will they entice those students intrigued by the possibilities, but fearful of the costs to their professional reputation. Given the risks of marginalization, why embark on this venture? There are scientists who believe that performative work is not serious enough, too ideological, and filled with fluff, and that it will destroy public confidence and reduce federal funding for science. When scientific undertakings begin to look like artistic expressions, they argue, it is cause for alarm. Why, then, should one enter this dangerous space? Before we embark on our "case studies," then, let us describe our journey into this field.

In chapter 1 we want to share two "intellectual biographies." We do so in the hope not only of making performative work intelligible, but also of demonstrating its essential place in social science. In this chapter we describe some of our earliest interests in allying arts and science, and then turn to the major intellectual watershed from which our explorations into the performative were launched. This watershed often goes by such names as postmodernism, poststructuralism, postfoundationalism, and post-Enlightenment. For us this transformation was captured by the concept of social construction. In chapter 2 we take a brief look at spirited developments taking place in performance art, performance studies, and in the social sciences themselves. This work has not only invited us to take risks, but is also having a catalytic impact in the social sciences more generally. Finally, in chapter 3, we pause for reflection. Here we outline some of the major ways in which we believe a performative approach both enriches and expands the potentials of social science.

1

Shifts that Launched a Thousand Faces

Recently we had the good fortune of visiting Zurich's Museum of Modern Art accompanied by an artist friend, Regine Walter. One of the most arresting exhibits of the day proved to be a video installation. The film depicted the dance studio of a Muslim immigrant residing in Switzerland. The instructor and his wife were busy teaching blond Swiss children how to dance to American hip-hop. The film not only undermined stereotypes of Muslim immigrants, but also explored the dislocations of people and images in the modern world, and the ironic fusions of radically different cultures. Yet Regine was not happy with the presence of the work: "What is this video doing in an art museum?" The question was particularly important to her, as her professional life has been devoted primarily to the traditional craft of painting. In a sense, the film constituted an alien invasion into a sanctuary reserved *for the arts*. The film was indeed unremarkable in terms of aesthetic craftsmanship. However, as an ethnographic documentary, it was outstanding. Why should an ethnographic study—traditionally the property of the social sciences—be featured as "modern art"? The opposite question was equally provocative: why are paintings—and indeed theater, music, dance, and the other arts—systematically excluded from most scientific work? If art museums can feature work of broad social relevance, why shouldn't social science journals and books include artistic work?

In our view there is a set of debilitating binaries operating here, one that equates science with reason, truth, objectivity, and progress, and the arts with emotionality, artifice, subjectivity, and entertainment. As such binaries have come to dominate professional life, there has been an unnecessary distancing between classes of pursuits that might otherwise draw enormous sustenance from each other. Decades ago, C. P. Snow (1993) described the yawning gap between the cultures of science and the humanities. He decried the fact that the two cultures knew so little about each other. How much could be gained by developing more artistically informed sciences and more scientifically sensitive arts? There are instances when this has been accomplished. The novels of Dostoevsky and DeLillo, the art of Edward Hopper and Barbara Kruger, the statues of Vigeland and Brancusi, the plays of Pirandello and Beckett, the photography of Diane Arbus and Walker Evans, and the music of Shostakovich and Woody Guthrie are scarcely "mere entertainment." Many find in their works deep truths about the human condition. And is there not enormous beauty in such simple, but encompassing formulations as $E = mc^2$ or the figure of the double helix? The technical drawings of Leonardo Da Vinci are beautiful, and photographs of the earth from outer space breathtaking. Why, then, the separation? Could it be otherwise?

We entered our careers in psychology with a long history of enjoyment and deep respect for the arts. In our idle hours we sometimes trace the beginnings of our interest in the performative to the movies. We both grew up in small towns encumbered by rigid conventions and omniscient surveillance. Then, there were the Saturday matinees! There in the dark, out of sight, new worlds sprang to life, from out of history and from around the world. We were intoxicated by heroes and villains, tap-dancing damsels, high romance, daring deeds, and mysterious events. At the film's end, we exited to a world of bland and predictable order. Over the ensuing years we became variously engaged in painting, dance, poetry, music, and theater. All these experiences carried echoes of those early epiphanies. As they suspended "what is necessarily the case" and played at the edge of possibility, we were enthralled. As we later launched our careers in psychology, we found that the exciting worlds of the imagination were treated as not only irrelevant, but also counterproductive. The discipline was indeed disciplining. But we did survive, as we found two important resources that offered hope for blurring the borders between science and art.

THEATRICAL STAGES OF OUR LIVES

Both of us entered the field of psychology for two important reasons. First, we were fascinated by the social world, its dramas, ironies, conflicts, creative potentials, and so on. Second, we wished to master the means by which we could contribute to knowledge that might make for a better future. We were eager to absorb all that science could tell us and learn how to engage in research that would increase this storehouse of knowledge. In both these respects, graduate education was deflating. First, what did the field have stored up in the way of nourishing knowledge? Virtually nothing. Almost every proposition about human behavior was either contested or banal. Moreover, there was a yawning gap between the abstract propositions about people's actions and our daily life experiences. Where in the rough and tumble of daily life were we to locate an "anticipatory goal response," a "cognition," "generalized arousal," and so on? The methods of research added to our dismay. We set out to do research with ideas that were intriguing, but as we began controlling variables, maintaining constancy across conditions, developing numerically based measures, and reducing all variation to mean differences between groups, the life was slowly drained from our ideas. In contrast, in reading a novel or watching a film we often found ourselves enthusiastically nodding, "Yes, this is so right," or "Yes, this is the way it could be." What if something closer to an aesthetic engagement was the essential ingredient of knowledge-making?

These thoughts were further sustained when we considered how interesting it was to look at daily life as theater. This view can be traced at least to Shakespeare's metaphoric "All the world's a stage." However, what proved most useful for us was the work of role theorists in sociology. In its earliest stages, role research focused on the way in which people occupy structured roles in society (e.g. manager, mother, judge). However, for us such inquiry suggested an all too stabilized world. It was our friend Erving Goffman who in *The Presentation of Self in Everyday Life* (1959) most notably illuminated the micro-negotiations of identity that characterize everyday life. For Goffman a subtle gesture, turn of phrase, or a tone of voice served to create and manage one's identity. By the same token, others were free to penetrate the guise and reveal its artifice, thus throwing one's authenticity into jeopardy. In effect, individual life was a form of art, and as in the theater, there could be both good and bad performances. In our view, the dramaturgic metaphor colored Goffman's life in significant ways, as suggested by one page of our history with Goffman:

> It was the mid-70s and we thought it might be fun to put together a Rites of Spring party at our home. We invited Goffman, in part because we thought he would find the invitation amusing. He lived at some distance, so we had little expectation of his actually attending. Yet, as the party went into high gear, there was Erving at the door. As with the preceding guests, a maiden greeted him and interviewed him on his sins of the past year. This challenge appeared to propel him into an identity "game" that persisted throughout the evening: he became an evangelical minister! Later we noticed that he was engaged in conversation with a young faculty wife. But suddenly, to our shock we realized he was trying to save her soul! We lost track of his whereabouts after that, but at the party's end we spied him pursuing the young woman up the path to her car, demanding to know if she had been saved. She did manage to escape, leaving behind a shoe and an erstwhile minister.

There was no topping Goffman for puckishly unsettling social conventions. By the same token, however, Goffman's theater of life was short on dramatic narrative. His plot lines were sparse—limited to the here and now—and role negotiation was continuous. It is in this respect that Victor Turner's work was important. In his 1977 work, *The Ritual Process: Structure and Anti-structure*, Turner developed a view of cultural life in which actors collectively participated in playing out archetypical dramas. These deep cultural dramas often pitted forces of the good against evil—or structure against anti-structure. For him, the theater of daily life carried the traces of centuries past. The tendency toward structure was a universal outcome of the necessity for cultural norms. As norms develop, proposed Turner, they generate tensions; certain activities are forbidden, deviants are rejected or punished, and creativity is stifled. The tensions, in turn, generate antagonisms in which issues of good and evil are dominant. As the antagonisms are resolved or the conflicting groups are reconciled, there is celebration. For Turner, such celebrations become cultural rituals, and give honor to peaceful resolutions.

The metaphor of life as theater played an important role in our own daily relationships. On the positive side we began to see that emotions that once seemed altogether natural—such as anger, jealousy, irritation, and depression—had a theatrical quality. We had seen them enacted on the stage, in films, and on TV, so we knew how and when to do them. If they were a form of role-playing, we concluded, they were essentially optional. They were denaturalized; we could do them or not. In fact at one point we spent almost a year in crafting alternatives to anger, such that anger would cease to disrupt our relationship. We still benefit from that exploration. More difficult to handle, however, were the positive emotions—love, admiration, joy. To treat them as enacted seemed to empty them of authenticity. Sure, we had watched hundreds of performers utter the words "I love you," or the like. But you don't want to be conscious of this fact when you say this in daily life. We labored over this issue; we still do. However, we took heart in the possibility that if we both recognized the theatrics in our expressions of affection, it was precisely in the shared recognition that we were authentically intimate.

And what about us as scientists? Aren't we also playing roles, acting within longstanding and well-known conventions? A scientist must learn how to do it, how to speak with confident authority and raise telling questions about the work of one's peers. Even psychological experiments are crafted theatrical events. They require a careful setting of the stage so that the behavior of the subjects will eventually provide a successful ending to a story. If the story is a good one, it will carry intimations of good and evil. Scientists will silently "boo" when the villainous subjects in an experiment obey, conform, exploit, or reveal their prejudices; and will privately rejoice when those with high self-esteem or advanced moral reasoning do good things.

We recall the account of a graduate student at Yale in the 1950s. Major battles were being fought between two theories of learning, one viewing behavior as the result of environmental reinforcement, and the other as the outcome of the cognitive capacities of the organism. Or, as a sub-text, are human beings the mere puppets of environmental inputs, or do they have capacities for autonomous behavior? It was further believed that these competing theories could be tested against each other by observing the behavior of rats finding their way through a maze under varying conditions. As the research was taking place, graduate students would gather in the laboratory to gaze at the busy rats. And, depending on their specific turns at a choice-point, would applaud or agonize as their "pet" theory was affirmed or denied.

And finally we must ask whether our own challenging of tradition over the years wasn't living theater. How many times have we cheered the underdogs as they valiantly fought against the powerful forces of oppression? Weren't we casting ourselves in this role, and hasn't this injected energy into our efforts? Fantasy as vitality.

AMBIENT ILLUMINATION: VISUAL KNOWLEDGE

We were restless in those early years. Clearly there was more to knowledge about human action than the dry and distant accounts crowding the texts of the field. Couldn't an artistic sensibility add a vital dimension to the human sciences? An answer began to form as we took a broader look across the social sciences. In particular, sociology and anthropology seemed to have promising ventures in the making. In both fields researchers were making substantial use of visual images—both photographs and film. In sociology there was a small but flourishing field of *visual sociology*, in which scholars relied largely on photography to concretize what otherwise might stand as an abstract and often technical description. It is one thing to read a treatise on "southern poverty," and quite another to be jolted into consciousness by a set of photographs of people living in the actual conditions. As visual sociologists had realized, photographs can do far more than illustrate abstract ideas. They can carry an enormous amount of information and with more impact than a verbalized report.

There is more. When we read a scientific account of let's say drug addiction, the subjects of the account remain at a distance. They become objects for our inspection. However, when we look at photographs of addicts, we are drawn into personal relationships. We ask ourselves, are these similar to people we know, could I be one of these people, how could one let oneself sink into such conditions, and so on. We are affectively drawn into the issue, and the distance between them and us is reduced. Moreover, such images are often saturated with value. We want to do something about the situation. The photos add to the bland scientific statement of "what is the case," a more rousing invitation action. Recently we were drawn to Cathy Greenblat's *Alive with Alzheimer's*. Greenblat (2004) challenges the view of Alzheimer's patients as drearily drifting toward death. In a series of eighty-five photographs she communicates in an emotionally powerful way that the Alzheimer's patient is far more than a patient, and shows us how such patients can thrive in many ways. One of our favorite photographic books, *Incurable Romantics*, is the handiwork of a close friend, Bernard Stehle (1985). In his work he pictures people whose handicaps might seem to prevent them from romantic relations, but who find intense and meaningful love affairs. His photos communicate so much more than an abstract account of "mate selection among the handicapped." We feel with them; for a moment we are them.

Such work also blurs the line between sociological research and professional photography. One might suppose that the chief difference between these photographs and such well-known photographers as Walker Evans and Cartier Bresson lies in the quality of the photographic workmanship. Yet, art museums display a variety of photographic works in which the techniques are rudimentary. Sometimes the photos are simply Polaroids. It is the human significance of the content that counts. Photographs of Afghan women who have been shamed by sexist conventions to set fire to themselves and images of mutilated Marines from Iraq command our attention. If the message is powerful enough, the border between reportage and art becomes insignificant.

Visual sociology has developed and expanded over time in important ways. For one, increasing use has been made of film, which also opened the possibility of reaching a far greater public. Here sociologists have found allies in the burgeoning field of documentary film. As the work of filmmaker Frederick Wiseman made clear, fascinating, informative, and moving portraits could be made of life inside an urban ghetto (*Cool World*), a hospital for the criminally insane (*Titticut Follies*), or a ballet company (*La Danse*). And such films could attract broad and sometimes commercial audiences. Sociology, art, and film journalism can all converge, and no one cares to tease them apart.

Our interest is also piqued by the way some contemporary scholars focus on the visual dimension of social life. Their research focuses on family photographs, drag costuming, sports photos, adolescent artwork, billboards, graffiti, and so on (see, for example, Dikovitskaya 2006; Mirzoeff 2002). Again, this work shows that visual performances are a language, and one that is not readily translatable into text. The style of our clothing, the messages printed on our t-shirts, the labels on our jackets, and so on, are all communicating. Photographic records do not only "tell us about" these communications, they also draw us into the act of interpretation. The best means of understanding the language of images is essentially by immersion in the forms of life of which they are a part.

We were also inspired by developments in the field of anthropology. Since the early 1900s, ethnographers had made use of film recordings of life in other cultures. Pioneers such as Margaret Mead and Gregory Bateson brought ethnographic film into the mainstream (Bateson and Mead 1942). With the development in 1958 of Harvard's Film Study Center at the Peabody Museum of Archeology and Ethnology, the future of academic film-making was secured. To see a ritual celebration from Africa or Asia is far more informative than reading a description. Interestingly, some visual anthropologists avoid voice-over commentary on what the viewer is seeing. They want full immersion in the experience without the intrusion of a verbal frame. When we first discovered these resources, we could well imagine images eclipsing text as the major form of anthropological knowledge. Jennie Livingston's fascinating depiction of queer and transgendered ball culture in *Paris is Burning* played to enthusiastic audiences throughout the country. It also stands as a pivotal contribution to urban anthropology. Scholarship as visual image.

We are also thrilled by the contemporary development of "sensory ethnography," a study of the full dimension of experience. Visual ethnography introduces us to what can be seen in a given culture, and this is no small matter. However, sensory ethnographers expand the terrain of possibility beyond the visual dimension. For example, what are the sounds that various people experience in everyday life—not only the music (as in ethnomusicology) but the voices, the noise, the signals, the silences? From sight and sound it is but a short step to include touch, taste, and smell in the anthropological exploration (see especially Pink 2009). As Schneider and Wright (2006, 2010) propose, anthropologists and artists can not only learn much from each other's practices, but fusions of the two professions can also open new avenues of inquiry.

Yes, fusion of the two professions. That's what it is all about. Especially in the social sciences, where our major offering to the world is human meaning. Should we not use every resource available to us for creating and sharing meaning? These early flirtations with drama and image were important to us. However, it was another and more substantial shift that gave birth to our performative adventures. Here to tell about it is Ken.

THE RIGHT TO REALITY: CRISIS IN CONSTRUCTION

My days at school—from the first grade through graduate school—were stuffed with "is." This *is* true, *is* the correct answer, *is* good reasoning, and so on. Knowledge could be laid out in so many propositions. Education was about mastering the propositions. By the time I reached graduate school, I had accumulated a treasure trove of *is's*. I was fortified for the future. Then I met Sigmund Koch, who taught history and systems of psychology. With his satanic beard, penetrating glance, and curious speech— sardonic, ironic, comic—he proceeded to jettison all the solid certainties we had so devotedly acquired. What arrogance—but how fascinating! The anxiety over the loss of certainty was more than compensated for by the giddy sense of freedom from the constraints of "what is." I did not seek to emulate Sigmund Koch in my professional life. However, I did absorb him as a silent interlocutor, a treasured voice of cantankerous query.

My early professional years were marked by doubt in the traditional conceptions of knowledge and methods of research. Both Mary and I continued to march in the empiricist army of truth, while carrying with us a lame foot, resting in the arts. We longed for full usage of our limbs. Yes, the visual practices in anthropology and sociology were inspiring; they began to open the way. But we lacked a rationale, and more specifically we lacked the kind of philosophy of science that seemed to provide such solid foundations to the empiricist program. What kind of legs could we stand on; we had little but our whispers of doubt. We needed a very loud voice.

With the silent nudgings from Sigmund Koch, I began in the 1970s to ask impertinent questions about the science in which I was involved. I had a tenured position and thus the safety of critical reflection. So I published an article (Gergen 1973) that challenged the idea that social science knowledge accumulates, as in the natural sciences. As I proposed, no matter how careful and sophisticated our research, it does not seem to tell us about human nature—that is, about what people must necessarily do as human animals. Rather, it primarily gives us glimpses of cultural life at a particular time in its history. Further, I proposed, because our research is loaded with values, its dissemination can change the culture. Terms such as conformity, prejudice, aggression, and obedience, for example, carry negative connotations. And the way we write about them will typically paint such activities in negative terms. To learn about such research is potentially to absorb these values. Because of these *enlightenment effects*, as I called them, the social sciences influence what is the case, thus ensuring that social science knowledge is forever undermined. Understandably perhaps, my colleagues responded defensively. The article became the subject of broad controversy, only to meet with ultimate suppression by mainstream psychologists. There is a lesson here for the young reader embarking on performative work: do not expect your colleagues to embrace your endeavor. Many won't.

As for me, I learned a great deal from the arguments used against me. Mainly, I learned that the defenses of the empiricist tradition not only were weak, but when placed under scrutiny they revealed even deeper problems. In exploring these, I also realized that a major storm was brewing in academic life, one that centered on the concepts of knowledge, truth, and reason. There are many ways of talking about this period of transformation. It has been common to speak, for example, of the "science wars" and the "culture wars." More formally, the terms postfoundationalism and postempiricism are used, and, most popularly, postmodernism. For me, it meant a vital expansion in intellectual companionship. From philosophy I was inspired, for example, by Wittgenstein, Austin, Davidson, and Harré; from the history of science by Kuhn and Feyerabend; from anthropology by Geertz, Shweder, and Lutz; from sociology by Berger, Luckmann, Latour, and Garfinkel; and from literary criticism by Derrida and Fish. And then there were the absorbing works of Foucault, Gadamer, McClosky, White, and a host of others. Those were hot times! This is not the place for recounting the changes in my views resulting from these dialogues. The interested reader can take a look at my books, *Toward Transformation in Social Knowledge* (1982), *Realities and Relationships* (1994), and *An Invitation to Social Construction* (2009a). I will limit myself to the three conclusions emerging from these dialogues that were absolutely pivotal for Mary and me in terms of our commitment to performative work. They not only served as major critiques of the empiricist tradition, but also provided the much-needed alternative to empiricism. For us, this alternative falls under the rubric of *social construction*. There is much to be said about constructionism; here, my simple hope is to bring these pivotal conclusions to life, along with the adrenalin they inject into our performative efforts.

The Loss of Privileged Language

As an undergraduate I was fond of writing, and I had some success at it. I especially loved to "think poetically." As a graduate student my proclivities not only proved irrelevant; they were detrimental to my success. One must learn to write like a scientist—meaning among other things the removal of all sentiment, idiomatic expressions, and personal references, and the adoption of a flat, passive voice that ideally refers to observable events. As we were led to believe, this way of writing was more objective and unbiased than the "arty" habits I had brought with me. Here was a language suited, then, *to tell the truth*, unblemished by values or imagination. More formally, I was informed that good scientific language *corresponds* with what is the case. If there are thirty males and thirty females participating in my research, then to write "there were thirty male and thirty female participants" corresponds with the facts. It is this presumption of correspondence that allows scientists, unlike novelists or poets, to test their accounts against the world. If I write that the males in my study proved to be more aggressive than the females (as measured by the shocks they delivered to another person in an experiment), you can repeat the same study to verify (or falsify) my conclusions. The same could not be said, for example of the e.e. cummings' line

> love's function is to fabricate unknowness

This was all reasonably convincing at the time. But there were silent doubts. There was first the nagging question of a young psychologist: if scientific language is supposed to correspond with the observable world, what was I supposed to make of words that referred to mental events? I had never observed a "thought," for example, and had to ask myself, how did Descartes know he was actually thinking? We say that we have measures of cognition, motivation, attitudes, and so on, but how do we know that they are real-world events? And why are we confident that they exist while voluntary choice, or spirit—never mentioned in psychological research—do not?

Such doubts became more edgy when I began to think about the participants in our studies. We researchers had no trouble in claiming we "knew about" the behavior of those who participated in our research. We observed carefully and thoughtfully, it seemed, while they just went about living their unreflective lives. We could tell them that they had reduced dissonance, changed their attitudes, repressed their prejudices, and so on, while they had little clue. But what if we asked them? If they disagreed, whose account should we trust? This may seem to be a small and idle question, but it is not. Here we have what we take to be an observable world, on the one side, and a great variation in how it might be described on the other. Let's expand the case: You have just given a talk before a mixed audience, and as the audience files out they begin to discuss what they have observed about you. Let's assume they wish to be as objective as possible. A psychologist turns to a colleague and suggests that you may have attention deficit disorder; a fundamentalist minister tells his friend that you are clearly a sinner; a hairdresser tells his partner that you have last year's hairstyle; a fashion photographer tells her friend that you look "really hot." Here we have numerous descriptions, each favored by a different profession (and perhaps none of which you share). Further, the commonplace realities of one group are uncommon, irrelevant, or mythological to others. Psychologists will never consider "looking hot" as an attribute of the real world (though they may admit that it is part of the lay vocabulary), nor will they study whether or not a person has sinned. These terms, and we call them constructions, are not part of the psychologist's vocabulary for describing and understanding the world. On what grounds, then, can the psychologist claim any privilege in objectivity? One can't say, "Well, just go and look more carefully," because each profession would use its own vocabulary for "seeing." The minister is quite confident in discussing sin and salvation, but he is not trained to talk about the world in terms of attention deficit disorder, split imagos, dissonant cognitions, or most of the other terms making up the reality of the psychologist. By the same token, the psychologist will never observe the class structure so obvious to a sociologist, and the sociologist will not likely be interested in the profit motive central to economic science, or the selfish gene so central to the evolutionary biologist. And whom should we trust to judge which, if any of these descriptions, is the most accurate? Would the judge not be drawing conclusions based on his or her own professional assumptions?

The implications of this line of reasoning for social science research are profound. First, it removes the authority of any knowledge-making group to claim truth beyond its own borders of agreement. There are no theories or methods that are superior to any others in terms of depicting or illuminating "the nature of things." Experimental methods and statistics are no more objective or accurate in their accounts of human behavior than the interpretations of "the man on the street"—whether scientifically trained or not. They may surely be accurate in the world of psychology, but if you are interested in "sin" they are irrelevant or obfuscating. Most important, the researcher is no longer shackled by the demands of the formalized language within the discipline. Rather, in terms of describing the world, it is entirely legitimate to draw from the full range of genres, styles, dialects, tropes, and forms of communicating offered by our cultural traditions. In terms of accuracy, science is no more objective than a poem or a short story. It simply uses a different vocabulary.

But now for the radical expansion of the point: why written language? That is, why should our attempts to tell about the world be limited to writing (and speaking)? Why must a social scientist be limited primarily to *writing* about social life, as opposed to using oil paint, music, dance, theater performance, or any other form of communication traditionally associated with the arts? For many, such a question may press the boundary of credulity. Painting and dance indeed! This is not science. Or is it? Surely at the edges of scientific representation, we find the arts making an appearance. All scatter plots, graphs, maps, or diagrams are essentially aesthetic devices that convey information that cannot easily be conveyed in written word—if at all. And we have already touched on the impressive visual representations in sociology and anthropology. If the social sciences expanded the range of representational media further, to include the entire range of communicative possibilities available to the culture, would this not dramatically expand the potentials for illuminating the social world?

Lest all this seem a flight of fantasy, two caveats are required. The first is in answer to the critic who says, "This is absurd . . . Are you trying to tell me that a poem or a painting is as accurate as statistics in informing us, for example, about population differences between nations?" In this respect it is important to note that while there are no words (or any other expressions) that uniquely correspond to the world as it is, we can create a correspondence between words and reality *within a given community*. For example, there is no mental illness in the world except within communities (such as the psychiatric community) in which the participants agree that a certain behavior is a sign of mental illness. Other communities might simply call the behavior "weird," or "with God" (as the Irish would have it), while in still other communities the behavior would not even be noteworthy. So, if you have community agreement on what "population differences" means, you can say that statistics are more accurate than a poem or painting. But there are also communities in which Picasso's painting, *Guernica*, is a more accurate a depiction of the German bombing of the Basques than a statistical count of the casualties.

A response is also needed to the critic who says, "Science is about prediction and control, and to this end the arts contribute nothing. With scientific tools we can classify illnesses, for example, make predictions about their effects, and generate cures. Songs and dances are scarcely equivalent, and would interfere with the business at hand." The most important point here is whether the only—or even the central—task of social science is to make predictions. Darwin's theory of evolution has been of striking significance to Western culture, although it makes no predictions at all. And although the theories of Marx and Freud did make rough predictions, these were marginal in terms of the significance of those theories in cultural life. So, let us consider the potentials of the social sciences in a broader light. Putting aside the aim of prediction and control—which indeed many social scientists find deeply troublesome—what aims are worth pursuing in the social sciences? I suspect that the most common replies would include: generating a sense of understanding, providing new and useful insights, liberating people from flawed or debilitating beliefs, creating useful practices for society, and achieving political and morally significant goals. When considered altogether, the social sciences seek to add to the potential of humankind to improve life conditions.

In these terms, the chief question is whether adding a performative dimension to social science inquiry can further expand its potentials.

From Observation to World Construction

If science loses its privilege as the sole source of authoritative descriptions, the door opens wide to the performative. For me, this was a truly exciting development. The stage was also set for a second major drama. To appreciate what's at stake, consider another common assumption within the traditional view of science: we gain knowledge primarily through observation. That is, scientific knowledge depends on astute observation of the world as it is, uncluttered by biases of any kind. Or, ideally, the world should dictate our accounts of it. Yet, we have already seen that reality makes no necessary demands on how it is represented. We may equally use scientific jargon or a paintbrush in terms of accuracy. So, we may ask, what are we to make of our direct observation of the world? And, most relevant, is there a positive role for a performative consciousness in the process of observation?

Consider again the earlier proposal that different professions will have different vocabularies to describe things. Is it possible, then, that they will also have different ways of observing or encountering the world? Won't their attention be directed in different ways? As the seminal social psychologist Kurt Lewin once pointed out, someone on a Sunday stroll in the countryside will see a different landscape than a soldier looking for cover. But let's take psychologists themselves. If I were a behaviorist I would be interested in cause–effect relations. I would want to know how certain conditions influence a person's behavior. Thus, I wouldn't simply gaze at the person's behavior; rather, I would direct my attention to the *relationship* between the environmental conditions and the behavior. In contrast, if I were a humanist who believes in voluntary choice, I would not be so concerned with the relation between conditions and behavior. Nor would I be especially interested in the behavior. Rather, my attention would be drawn to the person's explanations of his or her actions, and particularly to the accounts of motives and feelings. In still another example, as a cognitive psychologist, my focus of attention would be entirely different from the behaviorist's or the humanist's. I would be drawn perhaps to the person's language, though not to its content (as in the case of the humanist) but to the way it is structured. In effect, what we observe is never unbiased; experience is deeply colored by what we bring to the situation. And what we bring is largely the result of the community of which we are a part.

Put in these terms, "what we bring" to the research is all-important. How we observe, what we find, and how we use the information will all be affected. This has both good and bad consequences. On the positive side, communities of agreement can make progress in their own terms. If we want to make predictions, then a behaviorist approach has its advantages; if we want to achieve a sense of mutual understanding, then the humanist approach is more helpful. And so on. On the negative side, when we embrace a given orientation we also lose our sight. We think only in its terms. Thus, our focus and our potentials as scientists are diminished. If the overall aim of the social sciences is to expand our potentials for living, a singular understanding of the world is strangulating. If scientific progress is not a march toward truth, but a matter of increasing possibilities for action, then maximizing our "ways of seeing" is imperative.

Now the door opens to the arts. What happens when we draw from the vast resources of the arts in terms of our ways of understanding? Let me share an example from my recent work with Mary. We were invited by an organization to make a presentation on the nature of dialogue. As it happens, there is relatively little social science theory of dialogue on which we could draw. Further, owing to their particular values and affinities, the organizers asked if we might somehow relate the topic of dialogue to the arts. A tough challenge. After some deliberation, we decided to invite the audience to join us in exploring the nature of effective dialogue through the metaphoric lenses of various forms of art. For example, if effective dialogue is akin to excellence in jazz, what would this tell us about dialogue? Here we were led into a discussion of synchrony, of moment-to-moment improvisation, and of the significance of practice. When symphonic music served as the lens, the conversation opened to such issues as complementarity and contribution of each instrument to the composition as a whole. Using the metaphor of painting, attention shifted to the novelty created by the combination of colors; a discussion of sculpting suggested concerns with the limits and potentials of the "material"—the metaphoric equivalent to one's conversational partners. Further dimensions of dialogue opened up as we considered dance, weaving, and theater. With each new form of art, the exploration was reborn, and new dimensions of understanding and appreciation emerged. By approaching the issue with various artistic sensitivities, the dimensions of dialogue expanded.[1]

Oscar Wilde was credited with the remark: "Before Turner there was no fog in London." Or, in effect, until the painter J. M. W. Turner used his talents to breathe wonder and mystery into these vapors, they were essentially unremarkable . . . simply there in the background of things. Similarly, one might say that Helmut Newton's photographs of women opened a way for women to feel comfortable and powerful in their nakedness, Andy Warhol's paintings helped us to see the aesthetic dimension of the ordinary, Bill Jones's choreography made visible the beauty in the movements of the physically handicapped, Le Corbusier's buildings made it possible to envision houses as machines, John Cage's compositions let us see music as organizations of sound, and so on. In Shawn McNiff's terms, "Art embraces ordinary things with an eye to the unusual and extraordinary qualities" (2007, 37). What exciting vistas open for the social sciences when the arts are added to our orientations to the world!

From "What Is" to "What Could Be"

A third major step now beckons. Throughout my early education in psychology, the challenge was to discover unflinchingly and dispassionately what is the case. Our task was not to preach about what people *should* do; this was for moral philosophers or religious zealots. Such views were all subjective in any case, just an interminable battle pitting some people's tastes or values against others. The important question for science was documenting what people in fact do. Ah, the holy grail of "is." The concept of *research* bears out these assumptions: one searches and returns to search again, with the presumption that with each return we can increase our knowledge of the fundamental order of things. The social sciences have fallen heir to such assumptions, with vast efforts devoted to exploring what are often characterized as fundamental psychological and social processes. But if to describe is also to create, what sense can we make of doing research on "the fundamental order of things"?

This traditional focus on "what is" also generates a strong tendency to sustain the status quo. There are pressures within most cultural groups to reach agreements on what is the case and this results in *realist* accounts of the world. Such accounts can be enormously compelling, so much so that one can scarcely imagine alternatives. What sense would it make in Western culture to deny the reality of disease, death, the brain, the economy, and so on? And yet, while useful in securing relatively dependable and effective forms of life, realist discourse is also debilitating. It begins to establish limits to our imagination, our patterns of living, our deliberations on the future. It mistakes our common agreements for universal truth. In this sense, in opening social science to performative engagement, we generate a much needed ballast to the deadening weight of the real. Imagination is again set free.

It is not simply that the focus on *what is* suppresses exploration of the worlds of otherwise. When we consider alternatives to the status quo we also confront issues of value. The question of "what might be possible" walks hand in hand with "what do we want?" What is valuable to us, and what do we wish for the future? It is just such questions that traditional research typically neglects. For example, traditional research on the way in which failure brings about depression does not raise the question of whether depression is a good way to deal with failure. This is just what happens, says the researcher, not what we want to happen. The same is true in research on aggression, mate selection patterns, norm formation, and so much more. As scientists, we don't ask whether it is a good idea for people to act in these ways. It is not our task to moralize; that is simply the way it is. Nor do traditional researchers often question the politics and moral implications of what they presume to be real. Researchers set out to study IQ, for example, without questioning its existence. And yet, the mere presumption of IQ creates a world of insidious comparisons. Much the same may be said for the common categorizations of mental illness, which may do far more to create mental illness than to alleviate suffering.

To be sure, many social scientists are deeply invested in moral and political issues, especially those concerned with achieving social justice. However, much of their work employs traditional forms of research and representation. The result of experiments, surveys, interviews, and so on are represented in graphs, statistics, and other traditional forms of professional communication. The passion for justice is there, but the message is largely muted by the use of traditional communication styles. Again, a performative consciousness can be a potent ally. Scientists can augment the traditional forms of research and representation with rhetorically powerful forms of writing, along with the full range of artistic means available for communication. Rather than being documented with a graph, injustice can also be dramatized, photographed, or sung. Each form of expression will add dimension to the message, enhancing its impact and its potential for social change. Each will speak to a different audience, thus bringing science and society into mutual orbit.

Many artists have shown how their craft can be used to build a different future. German expressionist paintings formed a telling critique of the rise of bellicose fascism; socialist realist paintings and photographs pricked public consciousness in their depictions of the poor; and the work of feminist artists fostered solidarity among women, to cite but a few examples. Today it is perhaps the world's youth who lead the way in using artistic forms for purposes of social change. With bold creativity and the help of the internet, they share with the world politically polemic videos; through remixing they intensify the messages; through cartoons they lampoon the otherwise mighty; through photographs and digital messaging they share and intensify scenes of injustice; through internet outlets in music and dance they join with companions across the cultural divides to foster friendship. If the social sciences are to play a significant role in society, it will not be through increased sophistication in their research methods, but rather through a multiplication in their skills of expression.

The fact that science could change the world by studying it was viewed as a fatal flaw in positivist research; for constructionists, it represents a major opportunity. From the charting of "what is," the role of science becomes that of creating "what could be." What world do we wish to create with our work? What is worth doing? When our professional activities grow from the soil of "ought," we are vitalized. There are few more exciting experiences in a scientist's professional life than fantasizing a future world, and feeling the freedom of expression to realize such dreams.

2

The Spreading Fires:
Ignition and Inspiration

To experience the freedom of expression in our professional work, to inquire and profess by whatever means available, engaging, and effective—what a source of inspiration this has been to us! Yet, given the freedom, how in fact do we proceed? What and how do we perform—when, where, and for what purpose? These questions still remain open, and we hope they will forever remain so. However, to move effectively we cannot move alone. The meaning and significance of our efforts will always depend upon our relationships, both past and present. In performative inquiry there are no isolated geniuses; whatever counts as genius emerges from a relational history and must be accorded this status. We look, we talk, we read, we absorb, we watch, we listen, we play, we are excited, we are exhausted, and we are supported—all with and through others. In this chapter we wish to share the relationships that have served as the chief incitement to our own performative developments—partly to illustrate the process of origination through relationship, and partly in hope that you, the reader, may find new companions here.

ART AS PERFORMANCE

For us the idea of combining art and social change emerged somewhere in the early swirl of political demonstrations—from civil rights, to women's rights, to the antiwar movement in the 1960s and 1970s. Many of the early demonstrations were disorganized and unruly; however, as political savvy developed, organizers began to understand these as staged events. Their impact depended on social visibility, and thus the events increasingly had to be prepared "for the media." Crafted rhetoric and organized action were staples for good sound and visual bites. It was only a short step to creating politically loaded "rituals" of resistance: vigils, chants, chaining demonstrators to building columns, burning flags and bras, and wearing dramatic garb. At this point, activism began to border on theater—an art form. What had been intrusive graffiti slowly morphed into Madison Avenue art. Hip-hop music moved from the ghetto to Broadway. Feminist and gay street performance became club showings. Performance art in America was coming into its own.

In the background there was the 20th century modernist conception of the arts as groundbreaking, opening new realms of experience and understanding. The conservative view of the arts as depictions of reality had been abandoned in favor of a view of the arts as vehicles for experimentation. One did not just compose music or paint pictures within the existing conventions, but experimented with new tonal or color combinations. There was romance in the idea of an artistic avant-garde. And with this shift, professionally trained artists also found they could use their craft for purposes of social critique and change. This was especially true in the case of German expressionism, socialist art, the antiwar art of the 1960s, and feminist art of the 1970s. Highbrow and lowbrow converged in exploring the power of the arts for social change.

There is no simple way to summarize these developments, as complex and chaotic as they were. There are a number of rich accounts available to the interested reader.[1] Much work took place in clubs, galleries, and on the street. Indeed, anyone at any time could generate an artistic "happening." The definition of "art" could no longer be dictated by "experts," but was now in the hands of the populace. Let us take another comic pause to describe a "happening" that happened to Ken in this early period:

> In the mid-1970s I was invited with the Philadelphia artist Sam Maitin to speak about psychology and art. The presentations were to occur in a local school. However, rather than simply accompanying the visuals with two talking heads, and inspired by the participatory art movement emerging at the time, we decided to generate an artistic "happening." Large white boards were located at the school entrance, and as the audience arrived they were invited to take up colored felt pens and contribute to a communal painting. In the adjoining auditorium, a rock group held forth an interpretation of the unfolding event, while colored lights blinked and danced overhead. The creative chaos was increasingly intensified until a moment in which, suddenly, all went black! The school's electrical system had blown its fuses. No light, no amplification, no colors—only an unsettled crowd trying to make sense of the dark. After some confusing minutes, the fuses were replaced. We

then turned our attention to discussing with the audience the definition of art and subjectivity, including the loss of light as a contribution to the artistic experience. At a reception following the event, an art historian from a nearby university launched into a diatribe, unleashing a torrent of verbal abuse. "You call that art? How dare you . . . ?" As I began to explain our rationale, the critic became increasingly incensed. Suddenly with fist flying he lunged forward to attack; colleagues rushed to restrain him. The times were indeed changing, but apparently with greater speed in some sectors of the art world than others.

Although chaos pervaded the emerging of performance art, it is possible for us to identify certain important landmarks. Very early we were enthralled by the work of Laurie Anderson. Her electronically modified voice, combined with instrumentation, and a collage of images generated mesmerizing performances. She was one of our earliest inspirations, and her recent work is no less so. While less world-bending, we were also drawn to the work of Spaulding Gray. His film *Swimming to Cambodia* combined biography, humor, ironic insights, and politically charged commentary against the backdrop of the bombing of Cambodia. Why, we asked ourselves, could scholars not move in just these directions—using the art of language in the service of social critique? Two other performance pieces that later moved us were *The Vagina Monologues*, Eve Ensler's feminist reclaiming of female genitalia, and *Exonerated*, a stunning theater piece by Jessica Blank and Erik Jensen. The latter work featured verbatim accounts of life on death row by prisoners who were later found innocent of the crimes. The performers sometimes included the ex-prisoners themselves, but the play also gave prominent actors an opportunity to perform the readings—which they did pro bono. Until recently, we could only see on film the work of choreographer Pina Bausch and her electrifying Tanztheater Wuppertal. Again, the borders of the craft were challenged, as she combined theater, surreal art, multiple musical genres, and iconoclastic dance movements, often in the service of critical social commentary. In one of her key works, *Kontakthof*, a large group of men and women in different sizes, shapes, and appearances performed repetitive movements over a period of several hours. Exploring the relation between the sexes, the "dancers" held and shoved, caressed, and tortured each other. Is this dance, critical commentary, or social activism—or does it matter?

There were others whose work we would occasionally encounter in more innovative museums. Central to our development, for example, was the sparkling array of feminist performers, including Holly Hughes, Valie Export, and Karen Finley. Though sometimes raunchy, their work often relied on a sophisticated conceptual background—just the kind so familiar to academics. Likewise, performance artist Marina Abramovic consistently challenged limits of our understanding of our bodies and of the separation between people. In one famous work, *Rhythm 0*, she placed her nearly unclad body in a passive position, and for six hours allowed audience members to act upon her using a wide range of objects she placed at their disposal (e.g. feathers, a whip, a rose with thorns, a loaded gun). Not only was the barrier between actor and audience challenged by the performance, but questions were also raised concerning our feelings about others' bodies. Other socially engaged artists have performed a striptease to the music of Schubert, explored everyday movement and its breakdown, interpreted a screenplay with improvised instrumentation, planted performers in the audience, had their bodies altered through plastic surgery, and installed a customized jukebox in a McDonald's restaurant. In resistance to the commodification of art by galleries and museums, many performers took advantage of one-time, chance occurrences. Politically active artists engaged in activities often classified as "guerrilla theater," further blurring the boundary between art and political activism. Everywhere traditions were challenged, barriers to what it is possible to say and do were removed, and new voices were added to the public dialogues. Why should this not also be so for the academic world?

We were especially fascinated by work that not only challenged traditional conceptions of art, but seemed also sensitive to the performative dimension. This seemed very much so in much early Dadaist and surrealist work, especially in the films of artists such as Man Ray and Salvador Dali. Duchamp's 1917 entry of "the fountain"—actually an ordinary urinal—into the exhibition of the Society of Independent Artists was a remarkably performative challenge to tradition. We found this same spirit in the later work of composer John Cage. His performances threw the definition of music into disarray, with works variously composed of a single note, the odd sounds of objects striking piano strings, or simply silence. The operatic compositions of Robert Wilson, although we could only watch them on film, also challenged our thinking. In his opera *Einstein on the Beach*, the storyline was abandoned, with the operatic "voice" replaced by movement (performed by a dance ensemble); the music was atonal and minimalist, and video often served as the stage-setting device. As we also felt, in their draping buildings, bridges, trees, and walls in fabric, Christo and Jeanne-Claude carried the performative spirit into sculpture.

Gone was the image of the alienated artist, hoping to capture in art the depths of human spirit. Here were artists whose work was an active force in changing the world. Again, we asked, why not scholars as well?

PERFORMANCE ENTERS THE ACADEMY

In this context of bustle and bursting of artistic expression, scholars began to focus on performance as a subject of study. Like performance art, the development of performance studies was chaotic and without clear boundaries of definition.[2] However, here too there were several shooting stars that captured our attention and expanded our consciousness. Like many, we suspect, a significant departure point was the collaboration between performance theorist Richard Schechner and anthropologist Victor Turner. As we mentioned in chapter 1, Turner was a major figure in generating a view of cultural life as performance. Schechner's studies of theater and ritual performances across various cultures were leading in a similar direction. Their relationship gave rise to Schechner's ground-breaking essay "Points of contact between anthropological and theatrical thought" (1985). Schechner's efforts subsequently gave birth to the Department of Performance Studies at New York University. This was a beacon institution in bringing together the arts and the social sciences, an academic sanctioning of the scattered efforts of scholars like ourselves. We were also fascinated and encouraged by Dwight Conquergood's efforts at Northwestern University, where he collaborated with others to generate multidisciplinary studies of performance (Conquergood 1982, 1989, 2002). Like Turner, Conquergood viewed ethnography as the study of cultural performances; but, most important for us, he added an important ingredient to performance studies, namely a concern with ethics and justice. For him, performance studies should be a center of social critique and political action. The same, we felt, should be the case with a performative social science.

Of course, performance studies did not develop as an isolated island. Its stirrings cannot be separated from other shifts in the intellectual climate. The drama of social constructionist thought was already sweeping through many academic arenas. Two other movements contributed to the new atmosphere, and they also fanned the flames of performance studies. The first is literary post-structuralism. Drawing from Saussure's early views of the arbitrary relationship between words and the world (1966), the semiotic analysis of plays and novels, and the idea of language as a self-sustaining system of signifiers, post-structuralism made increasingly clear that there were no necessary constraints (e.g. empirical or rational) on language use. One could play with the rules. One of our favorite rule breakers was Roland Barthes, and especially his autobiography *Roland Barthes by Roland Barthes*. This work is sometimes called "anti-autobiography," as Barthes writes about himself in the third person, and abandons the linear model of time that defines traditional autobiography. There is no beginning, and any life event may appear at any time. The later novels of such authors as Italo Calvino, Umberto Eco, Thomas Pynchon, Don DeLillo, Paul Auster, and Toni Morrison all drew directly or indirectly from the post-structural movement. And we thus ask, why should scholars any more than novelists be bound by the textual traditions of longstanding?

Closely related to literary postmodernism was a second major movement, one we like to call the *resistance of the marginals*. With constructionists and literary theorists challenging the idea that there is one right or true way of describing the world, significant questioning begins. Who is claiming authority in matters of the truth, and what political or ideological agenda is being served in these claims? For example, if there is no one correct way to describe history, then what right does any group of educators have to determine what histories must be read in the schools? And who is represented in these texts, who are the heroes, what groups are thrust into the margins? With this reasoning in place, minority groups of every stripe could begin to locate ways in which the prevailing accounts of the world—in both academic and media spheres—either erased their existence or represented them in derogatory ways (Smith 1999). Women, African Americans, Native Americans, and Chinese Americans, for example, found themselves largely absent from American history. Gay and lesbian, Latin American, and elderly groups began to reject the way they were portrayed on television and in the news.

As many argued, resisting the mainstream accounts also required resisting mainstream language; in Audre Lorde's terms, "The master's tools will never dismantle the master's house" (1984, 110). New languages, appropriate to the resistant groups themselves, must be sought. For example, French feminists Luce Irigaray (1985) and Julia Kristeva (1984) proposed that there is a woman's way of communicating that is pre-discursive, or realized in bodily expression alone. Others suggested that forms of art and music could be used to claim and extol one's heritage. Critique and performance were again allied.

With the writings of feminist philosopher Judith Butler, the move from the margins took an even bolder step toward performance. Her book *Gender Trouble: Feminism and the Subversion of Identity* (1990) had an especially important impact on Mary's performance work. As Butler suggested, gender itself is a performance; one doesn't have a gender, one *does* it. Thus, if social change is the goal, stereotype-breaking performances are required. Rather than capitulating to the dominant power—becoming what Foucault (1980) characterized as "docile bodies"—women can engage in resistant performance. Such performances will liberate them from oppressive conventions and open a space for new ways of being.

This logic was further carried into a range of new academic enclaves, including cultural studies, film studies, and media studies. Performance concerns popped up with increasing frequency. Most relevant to us and to many colleagues, such ideas began to challenge academic scholars to explore their performative potentials. For example, in a 1994 conference entitled "Unnatural Acts," at the University of California, Riverside, many of the presenters chose to "perform their papers." Accompanying these academic "papers" were dance performances, stage pieces, comedy, and the presentation of a chocolate pig cake. Such experiments in the humanities soon spread to the social sciences. Such were the silent supporters of our own madcap. These once small sparks of performance now give way to fireworks.

SPACE EXPLORATION IN PERFORMATIVE SOCIAL SCIENCE

Performance art and performance studies challenged and inspired us, and, perhaps most importantly, gave us the sense that we were not alone. When we first sipped the elixir of performance work in the 1970s, we could not articulate a compelling rationale for what we were attempting. It was somehow "in the air," and simply felt right. Yet somewhere in the 1980s, here and there, we began to find like-minded companions. Could this be a movement in the making? Not only were constructionist ideas beginning to take effect, but provocative work was also making more frequent appearances. Especially stimulating for us were the inventive experiments in writing in such works as Michael Mulkay's *The Word and the World* (1985), Stephen Tyler's *The Unspeakable* (1987), and Stephen Pfohl's *Death at the Parasite Cafe* (1992). Each was a courageous and innovative entry into the professional literature, at once serious and playful. Further, Augusto Boal's use of theater performance for purposes of political resistance opened new vistas of possibility (Boal 1979). Particularly groundbreaking was his reliance on "spect-actors," that is spectators who were invited to take part in the improvised unfolding of the drama. The divide between performer and audience was crossed, and the reverberations are still with us.

Inspired and encouraged by these various developments, in 1989 Mary decided to respond to a conference invitation at the University of Aarhus, Denmark, not with a standard paper, but with a performance. The topic of the conference was not irrelevant to the decision: postmodern psychology. The result of her presentation was rabid controversy: some audience members felt war was being waged against reason, while others welcomed the innovation with enthusiasm. Not to be outdone, in 1992 Ken was invited to give a colloquium at the Department of Psychology at Rutgers University. The topic was to be "Dialogic Processes and the Creation of Selves." Rather than presenting a paper in the droning monotone that typically characterizes such presentations, he used small performance pieces to illustrate his central ideas, adding an often humorous or dramatic twist to the conceptual issues. We were encouraged to find that our Rutgers colleagues were indeed open to this form of presentation, and the resulting discussions were lively. Then, in 1995 we organized the first symposium on performative psychology at the national meeting of the American Psychological Association in New York City. We had our doubts. Would there be an audience; would such work be judged as some strange and threatening anomaly? We were overjoyed to find the auditorium packed. We continued to mount performative symposia at the APA meetings for the next four years. Among the various offerings were plays, poetry, art, dance, comedy, mime, and multimedia presentations. All these performances treated issues relevant to psychological science.

One lesson gleaned from these early adventures was to expect the unexpected. For one, the unconventional character of performance invites audiences into unconventional responses. During one of Mary's erotically tinged performances, for example, an audience member chimed in with orgasmic shrieks. Moreover, performances themselves often demand improvisation. As an extreme case, at one of our symposia, two scholars with dance training agreed to give a dance interpretation of intimacy and alienation in relationships. At the last minute, however, one of the dancers had a death in the family and couldn't attend. His partner, Ilene Serlin, asked Ken if he could improvise with her. She then produced what might be described as a six-foot-long rubber band. With Ken stationed at one end, and relating as best as he could to her movements, Ilene danced—at one moment stretching the rubber encirclement to its extremes, and at another moving rapidly toward and around him. Intimacy and alienation in motion!

Let us share some of our most dramatic and painful moments of improvisation:

> The podium was arrayed with three connected tables covered with white tablecloths. Along with ice water and glasses, the tables carried the various equipments to be used by the five performers—a multimedia deck, books, a slide projector, a boom box, a television set, and more. Ken was the first performer, and his presentation required a musical accompaniment. The boom box was at the front edge of the table, so that the sound could reach the far corners of the room. As the music began, Ken felt the volume was set too low. He leaned forward to adjust the sound with his right hand, while bracing his body with his left arm on the table. Suddenly, with the weight of his body pressing forward, the front legs of the table leapt over the edge of the podium—carrying all

three of the tables with them, plus the water pitchers, glasses, technical equipment, the boom box . . . and Ken! To the gasps of the audience, he somersaulted over the tables, landing in a crash at their feet. Was he hurt, was this part of the performance, how could we go on? We did manage to pull things together, but the aura of chaos continued: after the therapist Peggy Penn read her poetry, the discussant, Stephanie Dudek, broke down in tears over the emotional impact of the poems. For some time she could not speak, and continued sobbing into the microphone. Another discussant, Ben Bradley, had to discuss Kareen Ror Malone's multimedia performance—while she waited for a technician to repair her deck and bring in a new television for her actual presentation. It was an unforgettable opening to the first performative symposium at the meetings of the American Psychological Association.

It was also during this period that we began increasingly to find ourselves with lively companions, colleagues who were also moving in congenial and catalytic directions. For example, in 2001 we were lecturing at the University of Pretoria in South Africa and were invited to attend a PhD oral exam by our host, Gertina Van Schalkwyk. To our delight, the "oral" was a theater piece: for her dissertation, the student had written a play reflecting her experiences working with schizophrenic patients in a mental hospital. The play was both touching and critical of current psychiatric practices. The audience consisted of graduate students and faculty members from three universities, and after the performance all joined in lively discussion. The discussion itself was included as a feature of the oral exam. In another case, Ken was invited to evaluate a "problematic" PhD dissertation submitted by a graduate student in a counseling program in New Zealand. The dissertation was composed of three different forms of discourse: a highly literate English version, an everyday English version designed for the public to read, and a version in Maori, the language of the candidate's family. Ken's reaction was enthusiastic; the dissertation was a milestone.

As a result of the APA symposia, we also had lively encounters with Lois Holzman, Fred Newman, and their colleagues at the East Side Institute in New York City. While the Institute had a significant Marxist history, its center of gravity had shifted over the years. The theoretical work of Vygotsky and Wittgenstein had become focal, the first emphasizing the social context of human development, and the latter the lodgment of meaning in relational action. For Newman and Holzman, human development could thus be viewed as an expansion of performative capacities—or, more politically, societal transformation is contingent on the expansion of our capacities to perform.[3] Newman himself was a playwright of some renown, having written over thirty plays. Short plays by Newman were among the most prominent contributions to our APA symposia. There in the bowels of Manhattan, the East Side Institute brought together a multidisciplinary, international blend of scholars, artists, therapists, and political activists. The Institute also sponsored a theatrical organization, the All Stars, which helped inner-city youth to both produce and perform in a large talent show. The talent show was enormously popular in the city, and later moved "uptown." Further, the Castillo Theater, attached to the Institute, continues to feature plays focused on social issues.

In 1998, we collaborated with the Institute to mount a full afternoon of performance work at the Arts Bank Theater in Philadelphia. We also invited the audience to participate, thus enriching the ways we might answer the question raised by the title of the event: "What Are the Possibilities for Performative Psychology?" In 2001, we and our colleagues at the Taos Institute joined with the East Side Institute to generate a multidisciplinary conference, "Performing the World." Although the conference was held at Montauk, at the far end of Long Island, we were flooded with applications to participate from across the country and from Europe. In one memorable piece, the internationally acclaimed artist Osvaldo Romberg showed a film in which the characters, transparent plastic humanoids, carried out complex and sometimes erotic relationships. The prominent organizational theorist, Frank Barrett, gave a jazz demonstration of the parallels between jazz improvisation and teamwork in organizations. Cultural studies theorist Caroline Picart gave conceptually rich lessons in ballroom dancing.[4] The East Side Institute has continued ever since to host this sparkling event.

In 2003 we also had the good fortune of a visit from Kip Jones, a recent PhD graduate from the UK. It was clear from our lively conversations that Kip would not follow a traditional research career. His vision of the future bristled with new and bold ideas, and the qualitative methods of the times were not sufficiently radical for his tastes. Performance clearly beckoned him, but how were his dreams to be realized in practice? At a 2002 psychology conference in Berlin, Kip presented an audio fantasy of a conversation between Klaus Riegel and Ken taking place in 1976, when both were joined in a revolutionary movement against the positivist paradigm in psychology. When asked to respond to the piece, Ken choked with tears in recalling Riegel, whose premature death left an unutterable void. More ebullient was Kip's later video piece *Thoroughly Postmodern Mary*, a "biographic narrative interview," as Kip called it. The piece did rely on collaboration, as it reflected Mary's responses to Kip's interviewing her about her life. The video ultimately included visual designs, photographs, text, and music. Perhaps his crowning achievement is the movie *Rufus Stone*. This professionally directed and acted film is based on Kip's research on the oppression experienced by older homosexuals living in rural England. Kip has been a major source of inspiration for performance work throughout Europe,[5] and has been unflagging in his support of our efforts.

Two additional relationships have been particularly energizing for us over the years, and we have learned much from them. Norman Denzin, whose creative energies we had long admired, and whose analyses of cinema and society were pivotal in the development of performance and media studies, is a major driving force in qualitative research in the social sciences and in fostering performative work (Denzin 2003). In their pivotal *Handbook of Qualitative Research* (2005), Denzin and his colleague, Yvonne Lincoln, have welcomed performance methods into the qualitative family. In their words, "Rather than privileging a single method or approach to the practice of inquiry, researchers are encouraged to use whatever techniques, strategies, and frameworks are required to conduct the best research possible . . . accounts that . . . are poetic, transgressive, unfinalizable, and transformative" (quoted in Kamberelis and Dimitriadis 2005, 44). In this vein, Denzin and Lincoln have encouraged researchers to become *bricoleurs*, working with whatever materials are handy and useful for their inquiry, and to "take on multiple and gendered images: scientist, naturalist, fieldworker, journalist, social critic, artist, performer, jazz musician, filmmaker, quilt maker, essayist" (Denzin and Lincoln 2000, 4).

It is thus that their *Handbook of Qualitative Research* (2005) has devoted chapters to performance ethnography, street performance, visual methods, autoethnography, arts-based inquiry, cultural poesis, and investigative poetry. These chapters advance ideas that are dizzying, provocative, evocative, and challenging. Denzin has also given performative work a prominent place in the programs of the annual International Conference on Qualitative Inquiry, which he hosts at the University of Illinois. The journals that he coedits, *Qualitative Inquiry* and the *International Review of Qualitative Research*, are among the most prominent outlets for performative experimentation in the social sciences. Indeed, in a special issue of the latter, entitled "(Performance is) Metaphor as a Methodological Tool in Qualitative Inquiry," the editors W. Benjamin Myers and Bryant Keith Alexander asked the authors to take on the challenge of creating metaphors to describe performance work (Myers and Alexander 2010). We especially appreciate the poetic power of Ron Pelias' contribution:

> Performance is an opening, a location—a curtain drawn, a wooden floor washed with light, a window that invites the voyeur, a circle in the square, a podium that stands before, an arena of play, passion and purpose. It is an opening where ghosts find form, linger, and haunt. It is an opening where eyes, with and without their consent, look. It is an opening where we find ourselves. (Pelias 2010, 173)

We must also add a personal note: without Denzin's support the present book might not have been written. In earlier years we had soberly confronted the possibility that Mary would not be promoted to a tenured rank at Penn State University. While her overall evaluations for teaching and service were stellar, and her publication record substantial, her writings were largely performative and qualitative. Her department of psychology was widely known for its strong empiricist commitments and "by the books" evaluations in terms of journal visibility. Among the external evaluations selected by the department was Norman Denzin's. As we later learned, his masterful account of the significance of performative inquiry, and the prominent place he gave to Mary for her contribution, was the single most important factor in her subsequent promotion. Thank you, Norman!

Besides Denzin and Lincoln, we have drawn enormously from the creative and challenging work of Carolyn Ellis and Art Bochner. We had brief but energizing encounters with Art in Philadelphia during the late 1970s. We lost touch when he left the area, only to realize in the mid-1990s that we were again in synchrony, especially since Art and Carolyn had found each other. The publication of Carolyn's groundbreaking *Final Negotiations: A Story of Love, Loss and Chronic Illness* (1995) not only gave birth to a new form of qualitative research—namely autoethnography—but made crystal clear to us the promise of social science writing as a literary adventure. Her recent novel *The Ethnographic I: A Methodological Novel about Autoethnography* (2004) stretches the ethnographic material into pure fiction. The written word in Carolyn's case is not simply an even-tempered, passively voiced report on the state of affairs, but a vivid and evocative vision of a life, now given to the reader as a gift. Ellis and Bochner had elaborated on the significance of writing as art in their 1996 work, *Composing Ethnography: Alternative Forms of Qualitative Writing*. In 1999 they also organized a conference on qualitative research in St. Petersburg, Florida (which was also the occasion for the resuming of our relationship). The conference placed a heavy emphasis on writing and performance work, and its outcomes can be found in Bochner and Ellis's edited work, *Ethnographically Speaking: Autoethnography, Literature, and Aesthetics* (2002). Carolyn and Art have been far more than intellectual and performative colleagues. Their friendship has been invaluable, nurturing, animating, and inspiring.

The social sciences are now alive with performative experiments; there is no easy summary to be made of such work. However, to share something of the spirit, the range, and potential of this movement as we have experienced it, we close the chapter with a brief account of some further contributions that have illuminated our skies. As we just pointed out, autoethnographies have become experiments in writing. In addition to Carolyn Ellis, we have been excited by Carol Ronai's account of her experiences as an exotic dancer/researcher (1992), Lisa Tillmann-Healy's dramatized meditation on her bulimia (1996), Lesa Lockford's classroom strip-poker escapades (2004), Patti Lather and Chris Smithies's multilayered collection of narratives with women infected with HIV-AIDS (1997), and Nicole Brossard's gender-blurring explorations of lesbian desire (2000). And lest we give the impression that this is a feminine endeavor alone, we might mention Marcelo Diversi's short stories of his encounters with Brazilian street children (1998) and the work of Bryant Keith Alexander, who writes about performance ethnography (2005) and as well performs (2000).

The performative shift in writing is also reflected in other fascinating experiments. For example, in a groundbreaking piece Karen Fox managed to juxtapose accounts of child molesting from three different perspectives by streaming them in three columns, vertically down the page (1996). Thus, the reader could follow the recollections and feelings of a victim, the victim's stepfather (then in prison), and Fox's own experiences, both as therapist and as victim, in a form that resembled a conversation among them. More recently, one of the most impressive movements in writing has involved poetry (Leavy 2009; Pearson 2009). Laurel Richardson and Elizabeth Adams St. Pierre offered a compelling rationale for this movement in their contribution to the *Handbook of Qualitative Research* (2005). Excellent exemplars of this development are found in Brady's *The Time at Darwin's Reef* (2003), Richardson's *Fields of play* (1997), and Mary Weems's *White* (1997).

Many experiments in writing cry out to be read aloud. This impulse led to the emergence of the new genre of *performance text*, that is a textual script intended for public performance: "Performance texts are not simple, confessional tales of self-renewal as much as they are provocative weavings of stories with theories" (Cho and Trent 2009, 1015). Some of our favorites include Carol Smith's *Hey Girlfriend* (2005), on doing research with women living in high-risk situations (e.g. HIV-AIDS, poverty); Hye-Young Park's screenplay in English and Korean exploring her son's rapid assimilation to a new country and accompanying loss of his skills as a Korean speaker (2009); and Goldstein and Wickett's stage adaptation of an investigative report on school safety (2009), which was performed for five hundred teacher candidates at a Safe Schools conference. Frosting on our cake includes the performance text of Mariolga Cruz and her colleagues, drawing parallels among their lives as Puerto Rican, Iranian, and Brazilian people (2009); and Shoffstall's invention of a series of characters, including the mayor of Chicago and a murdered man, to treat issues of violence and homelessness in Chicago (2009).

Finally, there are the fully embodied performances themselves. Of pivotal significance in our own thinking was the work of a Canadian group of medical and public health professionals who wished to educate doctors and nurses about what it is like to be breast cancer patients in their care. Patients with metastasized breast cancer joined in playing roles related to their own disease, and the production was presented in hospitals to the staff. The work was later published as *Standing Ovation* (Gray and Sinding 2002).[6] We have also been moved by the work of James Scheurich and his graduate students who produced a "research happening" designed to illuminate immigration issues by bringing audience members into interactive relations with Mexican immigrants. The happening included a movie, *Labores de la Vida/The Labors of Life*, illuminating the lives of migrant farm workers. Along the same lines, we have been fascinated by performance ethnography that tries to shake common understandings by involving the audience directly. In one case, for example, actors played the part of Mexican street vendors at an academic gathering (Alexander 2005), unsettling the common conventions and drawing the audience into conversation. It did not surprise us at all to find autoethnography as a form of writing slowly giving way to fully staged performance. We count ourselves fortunate to have seen Johnny Saldaña, professor at Arizona State University, transforming a story from his adolescence as a band member into a theatrical piece called *Second Chair*. This drama of "coming out" is also accompanied by his music.[7] We also admire the work of Tami Spry, who teaches performance studies and communication theory at St. Cloud State University. Tami's autobiographical and autoethnographic performances are emotionally charged explorations of gender violence, mental illness, race relations, and more (see Spry 2001).

Performative social science is slowly coming into its own. To illustrate the inroads it has made from its early beginnings, let us close with one of the most audacious performance pieces we know: Zoë Fitzgerald Pool's PhD dissertation (in 2008) from the University of Bournemouth. The dissertation arrived for Mary's review in a wooden box inscribed with a brass nameplate. In the box were placed two books, each page illustrated in colorful graphics, describing the outcomes of interviews conducted during the research. Also included were DVDs with visual and auditory expositions of this material. As appreciative gifts to the reader, there were an assortment of treasures: music, a mermaid doll, a large doll representing a stuffy old-fashioned professor, chocolates, and hundreds of tiny scrolls, each with a quote from the interviewees written in elegant calligraphy. Included as well was a map to describe how to "read" the ensemble, which was secreted into various sections of the box. There was no single way to "read" the dissertation. It was a cornucopia of possible experiences, rich and exciting.[8]

3

Playing with Purpose: Contributions of a Performative Social Science

We have now traced our steps into the performative world, and it is time for reflection. Looking back on this sea of excitement and activity, what can be said about the potentials of a performative approach? How can we explain why performative inquiry should be central to social science? Performative activities can be dangerous in many ways. Not only can young scientists' careers be threatened by the traditionalists in power, but the reputation of the social sciences themselves is at stake. After all, isn't it commonly held in our culture that the sciences should "stick to the facts?" No playing around with artistic stuff and no value biases! In this final section, then, we would like to review, expand, and elaborate on the major contributions of performative inquiry to the social science. These are not the only ends of performative work,[1] but in our exploration we have come to see such work as steps toward a radical expansion in potentials. When we add a performative approach to our work, promising new vistas appear, first in social inquiry itself, and second, in our relationships with the surrounding society.

ENRICHING SOCIAL SCIENCE

We entered graduate training with great aspirations and rich visions; we completed our training diminished in both respects. And as we began our careers as teachers and scholars, laboring under the publish-or-perish yoke, we wondered if our early vision had not been erased altogether. The social sciences are much the same today, dominated by an empiricist philosophy whose major goal is to document the world as it is. Armed with objective knowledge, the argument goes, we can form better policies and make wiser decisions about the future. As outlined in chapter 1, this view is deeply flawed and places arbitrary and injurious limits over our activities. This is not to argue for abandoning the traditional practices, but rather for removing the restrictions on theory building, methods of inquiry, and the potentials of the social science themselves.

New Ways of Knowing

We don't like to think of ourselves as perverse, but somehow we have always been more intrigued by non-traditional science than mainstream conventions. Sure, we have had our moments of enthusiasm in following the conventions; but behind the scenes, the work at the margins seemed juicier and more intriguing. We joined with colleagues in generating theoretical visions of the society, intended not so much to make "accurate assessments" of reality as to bring a special kind of attention to current forms of life and to open doors to new ways of being. We worked with critical social scientists in the analysis of injustice and oppression and joined with qualitative researchers whose major aims were to stimulate debate on social life, generate an empathic concern with the oppressed or forgotten members of society, and bring about social change. And through our work at the Taos Institute, we joined with scholars and practitioners with investments in generating collaborative practices in education, therapy, peace building, organizational change, and so on. In all these ways we were nourished and encouraged about the future of social science.

It is the emerging field of the performative, however, that opens an exciting new space of possibilities in the social sciences. In traditional research we approach the world with a set of theoretical ideas at hand. We search or scan the world in ways that may confirm or disconfirm these ideas. If we theorize about how this will cause that, we will observe a world of cause and effect; if we are interested in status hierarchies, we will find evidence aplenty of those. Yet, it is also clear that what we can draw from our careful observation will be limited by the ideas with which we began. A theoretically informed engagement with the social world is, in this sense, limited.

In contrast, by taking on the full range of artistic orientations to the world, the social sciences dramatically expand the way the world can be experienced and understood. If we approach the world with the eyes of a storyteller, we begin to notice unfolding dramas; if we approach it with a poetic sensitivity, we might notice subtle rhythms and cadences in speech; with a choreographic approach, we might see a world of relational patterns; with the eyes of a theater director, we might be drawn to varying character types; and so on. In effect, the performative orientation brings with it a vitally expanded array of "lenses for viewing," "invitations for dancing," or "canvasses for coloring," and with them myriad potentials for illuminating the social world. Merleau-Ponty once wrote, "The painter's vision is an ongoing birth" (1964, 190). The same potentials reside in all the arts and in their application to the sciences.

Inspiring Professional Engagement

We recall our graduate days when we watched "subjects" from behind a one-way mirror and rated their behavior on preassigned dimensions. If we were actually to meet the subjects, we had lines to memorize, so as to homogenize our personalities. This was good science, we were told; the results of the research would be "contaminated" if we had personal relations with the subjects. Then we set about transforming the behavior of the subjects into statistical data. Those too were robbed of personality. We then converted our experiences into dispassionate, formal, and often cryptic sentences. Slowly, the rich and engaging world of social life was reduced to antiseptic and alienating reports on distant others. Professional life began to resemble bookkeeping; concern for society was transformed into self-preservation in the academic marketplace.

With the development of a performative orientation, all that changed. Now we can give more direct expression to our passions. The first question we ask is not "what is true," but "what is worth doing?" This is a question of values—it regards the future we hope to build. And we are not hamstrung by a cumbersome and formalized language of representation, but can draw from our full range of potentials. In short, we are invited into inquiry that carries our visions and gives us full freedom of expression. The question is not whether this is science or art, but whether our professional work can help to build valued futures. It is difficult to know what this might mean for any given scientist. For some it might mean, for example, drawing from folk traditions woven into one's ethnicity, gender, or class. For others it could mean giving expression to one's aesthetic potentials—in writing poetry, acting, playing the piano, dancing, and so on. Traditional training in the social sciences fosters a disjunction with one's past life; the scholar learns to shed the "bad old ways" of understanding. In contrast, a performative orientation opens a space in which one's life experiences can become assets to expression. For us, it has meant all these things, and more. Perhaps most exciting for us is the way performative work urges us to take risks in becoming. To expose our values, to give them new forms of expression, and to do so before an audience—now that is passionate inquiry!

Building Community

As we have pointed out, traditional social science writing is not welcoming; it is difficult to penetrate, dispassionate, and impersonal. It is not easy to locate the authors as flesh and blood human beings. There is no indication of their feelings about the work; its personal significance to them; how it emerges from their hopes and fears, and so on. There is no expression of their values or political ideologies. Moreover, the demands of professional style require the writer to appear as a unified self. One must appear to have an "ordered mind," one in which all sentences exist in a state of logical coherence. As scholars we can scarcely admit doubts or misgivings in what we write. If we contradict ourselves, we are virtually disqualified. On the whole, it's as if social science writing should ideally be mechanical. Better, one might say, if the community of scientists were replaced by a network of robots.

Yet, forms of writing also generate forms of relationship. As we write these words, for example, we are also treating you, the reader, in certain ways. We are positioning ourselves as near or far, above or below, valuing your opinion or not, and so on. The kind of relationship invited by traditional scientific writing is depersonalized and alienating. It does not invite community, in the sense of a group of people who care, support, and nurture each other, but rather an organization of self-centered individuals forever anxious that their full humanness might be revealed.

When we enter a performative consciousness, all preceding conventions of scientific communication are suspended. All restrictions on styles of exposition are lifted, and the full range of human communicative activity is welcomed. This does not mean an abandonment of the old traditions, but a radical expansion in possibilities. Most important for the present, it also invites us to explore forms of expression that contribute to a community of caring. It is in such a community that we can more easily take risks, both in revealing the full array of our being and in exploring new potentials for becoming.

Sustaining the Creative Impulse

Beware Truth and Method. For when we have fixed the criteria of truth, and the means by which it is achieved, we have fixed the limits of imagination and action. Even with the growth of a constructionist perspective, pockets of consensus tend to emerge—for example, on what constitutes "good" as opposed to "bad" qualitative research or discourse analysis. The challenge, then, is to ensure that reflective deliberation is unceasing. Ambiguity is precious; certainty is suffocating.

In our view, a performative orientation continuously disturbs and disrupts. It prompts us to ask of any existing accomplishment, "Well, that's one way to do it; I wonder what else could be done." It is like having a starter dough for continuously nourishing the creative process. Experimental writing, autoethnographic performance, public theater pieces, and so on, all challenge us to think creatively and expansively about our activities. When such work appears in our academic journals, it opens new ways of thinking about those same journals: "Hmm . . . If they will publish that, I wonder if I can propose this strange idea." By the same token, a performance-based symposium at a scholarly conference, a performative colloquium, or a play used by students to incite discussion in a classroom, all transform the character of these sites. They challenge the conventional rules of thought and action associated with these times and spaces, and invite others to join in exploring possibilities. For us, performative work functions as a continuing catalyst for creative expansion, constantly pressing the perimeters of possibility.

SOCIAL SCIENCE AND SOCIETY

As we saw, the social sciences can be enriched in multiple ways through performative work. But this does not take us far enough. The issue here is not the enrichment of our lives as scholars, but what do we offer to society—and indeed, to the world. Of course, the more we can do within our disciplines, the more we can offer to the world; but we also know that a scholar can live a tranquil and successful life without offering the society much of anything. The fact is that the social sciences owe their existence to the surrounding society. Without a generally shared belief that the sciences contribute to the public good, their place in our educational institutions would be endangered. The question is: How does a performative consciousness in social science benefit the surrounding cultures? For us there are four significant contributions.

Expanding Audience, Enhancing Engagement

A major limitation of "good professional writing" is its limited audience. Most of this writing is essentially guild-oriented communication, designed for a specialized audience. And the specialty is scarcely the field as a whole—for example the discipline of psychology, sociology, or economics—but rather a subdiscipline. In the field of psychology, for example, there are over fifty-five subdisciplines, most of which produce their own journals. Reading across specialties is often difficult: the writing presumes understandings that are shared only within the guild. Even within guilds, the audience for any published work is usually small. The typical journal article in the social sciences will be fully read by fewer than ten people. Demands for economy in writing and absence of any passion make for dull reading.

Worse still, in communicating properly to our peers, we fail to engage in relationships beyond the scientific sphere. Here we have superbly educated groups of professionals, with time and often funds to carry out research and to write. Yet, the results of the countless hours that go into a research study are opaque to virtually anyone outside the guild. This inability to speak to the society doesn't go unnoticed. Our writings are frequently charged with "elitism," and the critique is on target. Seldom do the "objects of the scientific gaze" learn about the results of such research. Seldom do we scientists invite them to talk about our research and its implications for their lives. The poor, the minorities, the imprisoned, the aged, the deviant, the immigrants, the terrorists, and so on are essentially "out of the loop."

In contrast, with a performative consciousness we dramatically expand our capacities to relate. We can draw from the full range of the arts—using theater, film, or music, for example, or the full range of folk idioms so disparaged in becoming disciplined. From a performative perspective, there is nothing called "communication" that cannot be marshaled for inquiry and sharing. This is not a matter of "writing across the curriculum," nor even "writing across the society." It is ultimately a matter of communicating with full potentials to all peoples. A performative consciousness prompts our asking such questions as, "Who is this for?" "Am I being understood?" "Will this be meaningful?" "What can they do with this?"

Yet, more is at stake here than sharing alone. As we see it, performative work can greatly increase what we like to call *dimensions of engagement*. Here we refer to the various ways in which our communication engages an audience. For example, if we read an abstract theoretical paper at a conference, we hope that we can stimulate our audience intellectually. If we then share the reasons we care about the topic, revealing the passion that drives our work, the audience may join us in another way. In addition to intellectual engagement, there is now *affective engagement*. Listeners may come to care about what we are saying. There is more. What if we convert the piece into a theater, such that the ideas are embodied by actors? As people watch actors, they vicariously become participants in the play itself. Here we have *mimetic engagement*. Let's add again, let's say, a musical background to the dramatic piece, much as we find in movies. Such music often carries with it evocations; it creates a mood that can deepen the drama, in effect, a *contextual engagement*. By expanding the repertoire of performance, we also expand the potentials to engage our audience. We not only perform *for* an audience, but *with* it.

We must, however, sound a note of caution. A performative orientation is no guarantee of increasing either impact or engagement. Yes, we praise the work of social scientists experimenting with performative inquiry. Yet, it is also true that the major audience of much of this work—ours included—remains within the halls of the academia. And even here, some performative work will sing to your soul, while other offerings will leave you only puzzled. Opening the doors to performative work dramatically expands our potentials, but it does not guarantee the outcomes.

Enriching Dialogues between Science and Society

The two of us sometimes joke that if we can't talk about our research with the person who cuts our hair, we probably aren't doing anything significant. We laugh, but there is a serious side to it. Clearly, if the hairdresser can't understand what is important to us, then it will never be important to him or her. And if we cannot carry out a meaningful conversation, then we run the danger of living in a professional bubble. This is especially the problem when we are interested in social change. What arrogance to think that we in the social sciences should change people's lives, when we don't know them, don't listen to them, or don't reflect their views and values in our work. How much damage to people's lives, we ask, have the mental health professions done by defining problems in living as diseases—all in the interests of helping people? Our contribution to society should not be hierarchical, with all the content moving "downward" from "the top." If we are not in dialogue, our research becomes the byproduct of crude stereotypes constructed within isolated encampments. The main point here is that by using forms of communication that can reach society, we establish the grounds for dialogue. Traditional scientific writing speaks down to society; it positions the reader as ignorant. It also tends to be oppressive, suggesting the weakness of competing claims to truth. In contrast, when we communicate with forms of theater, poetry, film, or photography—all common in society—we can create a comfortable environment. People approach performance not defensively, but with an openness: "Show me," "Entertain me," "Intrigue me." Often they find a movie, a novel, or TV show that resonates with their personal experience, and that they want to share with others. Interestingly, when the East Side Institute presents a play about social justice to an audience, the end is not the applause at the curtain's close, but an animated discussion with the audience. A performative social science invites dialogue between society and science, but also within society itself.

Fostering Social Change

Earlier we made a case for the social sciences as world-making. Scientific accounts do not so much hold a mirror to nature as they create what we take nature to be. And these accounts can make a difference in what happens next. Here we must stress the word "can," because our traditional ways of describing and explaining are scarcely intelligible to anyone but scientists themselves. Or to put it more bluntly, our professional training leaves us culturally mute. In contrast, performative work invites us to pursue our passions, hopes, and dreams for the future, and therefore place our values in the forefront of our efforts. It is scarcely surprising, then, to find that most performative work to date is invested in issues of social justice, liberation, and empathy with people at the margins (see Alexander 2005). Further, performative work can expand the audience for social science inquiry, inject passion into its messages, and enable the audience to participate. In all these ways the potential impact of our research is augmented. In effect, when we add a performative dimension to the social sciences, they become a greater force for social change.

Revitalizing Society

Well-being in a society always requires a certain degree of stability. In our daily lives we generally sustain the ordinary—going to work, buying groceries, talking on the phone. It works for us. At the same time, in living normal lives we are slowly building prisons for ourselves. When things are just as they are—when this is true and that is false, this is good and that is bad, this is sense and that is nonsense—we close down our options. There is less that can be said or done, less that can be changed, less that can even be fantasized. There is a small death in the creeping of convention. At the same time, there is a strong deconstructive tradition in the arts. In Nietzsche's words, "We have art that we may not perish by the truth." When novelists create imaginary worlds, poets play with language, artists experiment with color, photographers take pictures from new angles, they are unsettling us. They disrupt the commonplace. It is no surprise that fascist governments move rapidly to suppress artistic creativity: even the smallest cartoon or a lampooning comedian can pierce the armor of state. Should the social sciences be any less powerful in their capacity to challenge the status quo?

Yet there is a subtler way in which performative work prevents death by convention. Such work in the social sciences occupies a liminal space: it is not quite science, nor is it exactly art. It is science with an artistic face, art with a scientific flavor. This very ambiguity functions as a disruptive force, challenging the traditional binary of science vs. art and inviting prescient pause. In Victor Turner's words, "Liminality is full of potency and potentiality. It may also be full of experiment and play. There may be a play of ideas, a play of words, a play of symbols, a play of metaphors. In it, the play's the thing" (1977, 33). In this sense performative work undermines the tendency to freeze realities. To be sure, performance pursuits may express a particular point of view, often passionately. Yet the very fact that the expression takes the form of play informs the audience that in spite of its power, the message is an artifice—crafted for the occasion. "It is serious, but it is not ultimate." Compare this with traditional empirical work, in which researchers do all they can to suppress the signs of subjectivity. They write from a god's eye perspective: "This is the way it is." Realism and rigidity walk hand in hand. As we see it, performance work does make declarations about the real and the good, but simultaneously removes the gloss "is True." Performative pursuits continuously remind us that everything remains open to dialogue. We are all included!

SECTION II

LITERARY ARTS: PLAYING WITH POTENTIALS

In learning to write like scientists, how limited we become! Any writing that smacks of art, the ordinary, the passionate, or the playful is considered illegitimate; the responsible scientist will be on guard against "frivolous" rhetoric. This suspicion of rhetoric is represented in Occam's famous dictum: "No unnecessary words." Good scientific writing is abstract, flat, and unemotional. Not only is it typically dull and impenetrable, but it also fails to communicate to anyone outside the discipline. Because the intellect of the individual scholar is at stake, the writing is also self-protective: in the name of "advancing knowledge" it attempts to appear superior to the claims of others. To be at the forefront of the field means writing in such a way that others are thrust to the rear. It is not the skimming sailboat that serves as the guiding metaphor of social science writing, but something more akin to the perfectly appointed gunboat—powerful in resources, flawless in operation, insistent on purpose, and beyond defeat.

It is now time to cast off the unwarranted demands of tradition, and to explore the full potentials of the written word in social science. In the present section we share some of our own experiments in writing and ponder their potentials. We explore the possibilities of duographic writing, collaging voices, entwining texts, multiple voicing, and more. We offer such explorations with humility. There are no gunboats here, but rather tentative experiments in crafting new forms of communication. If nothing else, we hope they will encourage others to traverse the walls of tradition.

4

Duographic Writing

Both of us have been involved for many years with the narrative movement in the social sciences. Concern with narratives is now burgeoning, touching virtually all the social sciences and humanities. In 1994, we were each invited by John Lee to write a biography for a book designed to reflect the lives of narrative scholars. For us, there was a certain irony in the invitation, as we felt that narratives created lives as much as they revealed them. Abandoning the traditional demand for an accurate account of our lives, we thus followed Roland Barthes's invitation to play with autobiography (1977). In particular, coming from a constructionist background, we were particularly concerned with replacing the traditional view of the lone author revealing his or her innermost thoughts with a conception of meaning as cocreated. How could we craft a form of writing that replaced the individualist ideology implied in autobiographical writing by "making real" our relational existence? We finally hit on the idea of the *duography*. As you will see in the excerpted account that follows, we give initial space to the traditional form of autobiographical writing. However, as we move through the offering, the individualist voice gives way to an unidentifiable author who writes about "we." Finally—and almost mysteriously—there is a full blurring of authors and identities. We also interrupt the narrative from time to time to reflect the historical context, thus incorporating it into the relational nexus.

LET'S PRETEND: A DUOGRAPHY

1965 . . . U.S. Troops Authorized to Fight in Vietnam . . . Race Riots Rage in Watts . . . Zorba the Greek . . . First issue of The Journal of Personality and Social Psychology . . . The Women's Room . . . The Miniskirt and Twiggy: New Fashion from England . . . The Graduate . . . Come on Baby, Light my Fire . . . Sergeant Pepper's Lonely Hearts Club Band . . .

Who Is That Masked Man?

Mary Gergen
It was the fall of 1965. Michael and I had just moved from Minneapolis to Watertown, Massachusetts, where he was enrolled in MIT's master's program in architecture. An architect friend invited us to a Halloween costume party. We hustled up some last minute "campus rebel" costumes, and arrived to find the basement rec room crowded with bizarre figures. As we descended the stairs, we were greeted by the hosts, who informed us that a contest was in progress to identify the psychological concepts that Ken and Eleanor portrayed in their costumes . . .

Saturday Night Shuffle: A Second Sounding

Ken Gergen
If one comes to a costume party "dressed" as the Id what is there to do but indulge the senses? And was I not eminently deserving of such indulgences, given my childhood days? To protect themselves against the untrammeled exuberances of four young boys, my parents—a mathematician and a cultured New Englander—had enforced an array of demanding rules of household decorum. I later added to these suppressions by developing a deep idealism, expressed—to my parents' dismay—in a youthful commitment to the Southern Baptist Church. Perhaps the culminating expression of self-bondage was a premature marriage to Eleanor—a very fine woman, but whose very virtues placed tight restrictions around all forms of deviance. Only the spontaneous energies of our children, Laura and Stan, provided a sanctioned form of impulsivity. And now the 1960s were upon us, and I was beginning to respond to their rhythms . . .

. . . Martin Luther King Shot by Sniper . . . France Nearly Paralyzed By Protesters . . . Bobby Kennedy Shot in LA . . . Soviet Tanks Invade Defiant Prague . . . Israel smashes Arabs in Six Day War . . . Police Battle Mobs as Democrats Meet . . . Vietnam Reds Launch Tet Offensive . . . Joan Baez Arrested in Antiwar Protest . . . Make Love Not War: 10,000 Hippies Rally in New York Be-In . . . Soul on Ice . . .

Exodus: A Road to Rome

Mary Gergen
It is late summer, 1968. Leaving New York on an Italian ocean liner with Ken and my two preschool children, Lisa and Michael, was a dramatic

and wonderful turning point in my life. Until that moment I was not sure that the fantasies and plans for a year in Rome would actually materialize . . . Had we listened to too many fairy tales in our childhood, or too much radio make-believe, or seen too many Hollywood spectacles? Was this life copying art, or as Woody Allen suggests, bad television? (Reflecting on our actions, I wonder now if our bold and ultimately wise decision did not give us the courage to travel a great many uphill grades . . .) In Rome our lives settled into a joyous routine. The trip seemed to have lingering effects on our lives—drawing us closer than ever. I no longer feared that I was disappearing; I could sense that I made an important difference to Ken. Somehow through me, he gained in himself. And I, through him, was growing as well. The partnership was establishing roots.

Another Ro(a)ming

Ken Gergen

A moment of epiphany—early afternoon in an olive grove, flat on my back, arms outstretched, regaled with fresh bread, cheeses, and grapes, sated with Frascati white wine and a tumble in the grass, with the spirits now drawn to the heavens by the towering pines of Hadrian's Villa. The previous months at Swarthmore, where I had taken the position as chair, were agonizing . . . For me, my family, and friends. The grief of separation had at last given way to a glimpse of heaven. But what was this "run to Rome" with Mary? Cinematic fantasy, a leap into the absurd, the firm footing of a new beginning? I hadn't a clue, but was hell-bent on the exploration. It was all so clear that I had a *mate* in the Australian sense—happy to hang with me atop a flee bag hotel in Athens (where one could also behold the Acropolis in the moonlight), bear up under the thunderous tone of a Tunisian cabinet minister as he lambasted American foreign policy (and us as its carriers), sleep in the crack between the only two single beds the four of us could find on the edge of the Sahara, stay cool as the hostile border guards at a renegade outpost in Algeria questioned our legitimacy, tough it out when our Fiat was in a small collision, which was settled out by a yelling Arab crowd in Marrakesh, and swear in Italian at the landlords who cheated us out of our deposit . . .

I wrote a small book that year, *The Concept of Self*, and dedicated it to "Maria at Hadriana" . . .

One of the most compelling features of this relationship was its potential for collective insanity. Either of us could place an absurd idea, image, or fantasy in motion. And rather than examining its impracticality, its costs, or its nonsensical nature, the other would actually treat it seriously—as an entry into a possibly reasonable universe. The whimsy might be embellished . . . But there was common reality aplenty. Oppression, suffering, and revolutionary impulses were everywhere apparent—and absorbing. Somehow the laboratory exploration of abstract theoretical issues no longer seemed so relevant. Academic exercises for an ideologically insensitive elite . . .

And over all, there was the constant sense of sadness and self-censure. My children . . . Their laughter and tears haunted me. We were torn from each other, and was I not responsible? The dozens of letters and carefully wrapped gifts could not assuage the despair . . .

Mankind Makes Its Greatest Leap: To the Moon . . . Thousands overwhelm Woodstock Festival . . . 250,000 War Protesters March in Capital . . . 567 Massacred at My Lai . . . Hair . . . Easy Rider . . . Midnight Cowboy . . . Zen and the Art of Motorcycle Maintenance . . . Steinem, Millett, Friedan, and Abzug Speak at Women's Movement Conference in New York City . . . Millions March at First Earth Day . . . Kent State Shootings Shock Nation . . . Jimi Hendrix & Janis Joplin—Drug Fatalities . . .

Homesteading in Heaven, 1969

Mary Gergen

Coming home, to a place I'd never been. I recall the first moments of crossing the Walt Whitman Bridge into Philadelphia. First the smell of the oil refinery, then the sight of rusted, damaged cars piled up in a gigantic nightmare of trash, then the flames of the gas tanks, the bleak dirty landscape of South Philadelphia, the constant aroma of filth. Then we passed the airport and the swamp (which today is a national treasure, one of the last remaining inland marshes) and then Chester—a town left behind by industrial sprawl. I secretly regretted every snide comment I had ever made about growing up on the Minnesota prairie. The bleak highway finally gave way to the oasis of Swarthmore "ville." The college itself was small, quaint, peaceful, and almost lonely with its sparsely arranged buildings settled along grassy meadows and walled in by forestland. Our destination was nearby in Rose Valley. We were too alimony-poor to rent a furnished house in Swarthmore, so our friends from the college, Molly and David Rosenhan, found us a steal: for $238 a month we could buy one-third of an eighteenth century country inn, where a stone wall and picket fence separated us from Possum Hollow Road. It was a crumbling affair with a Byzantine interior, but we adored it from the first moment we saw it. We were married here on October 4, 1969, with our children and few friends, Greek music accompanying, and a sociology professor/Unitarian minister presiding. It was a beautiful and joyous day as we exchanged the golden rings we had designed in Rome. The night of our wedding we slept in our two-person sleeping bag, which was to be our bed for the next three months. Our living room had no furniture for a year, but these were times when cushions on the floor were frequently preferred to chairs and couches. We had already had our honeymoon.

Outside our house, the world was in turmoil. It had a monstrous impact on the college: faculty and students were torn in many parts. (The President who hired Ken, Courtney Smith, had died of a heart attack during a sit-in in his office.) A Quaker school in origins, the campus was at the forefront of war resistance. Yet, many faculty members believed that civil disobedience and suspended classes were not the proper responses to the crisis. Meetings, strikes, antiwar demonstrations, and protests combined with a feeling of revolutionary high that had strong sensual overtones. Our major involvement was to develop a nationwide network of students and faculty to carry out a survey of college students, ten thousand strong, to document the negative impact of the war on the American university life. We tried to show that the protest movement was spurred on by the best and brightest of the generation, not by marginal, fringe, "hippy" types who were trying to evade their civic responsibilities. I worked in the trenches on this one, and together with Ken I took the findings to the public. We went to Washington to see the President's special advisor to the colleges, issued a press release that was picked up by *Time* magazine, and in the summer of 1970, while living in Minneapolis (where I had taken my new husband home to meet my folks), we tried to write a book about it. In the end we abandoned the project. Time was rapidly passing and world concerns were moving on . . .

Beginning Again

Ken Gergen

The challenges were enormous—a new marriage, a "new" but empty house, new classes to organize, and a politically explosive ambience. Campus life had taken on a surreal dimension. The student–faculty distinction was giving way; all were politically engaged, wore denim and love beads, and used phrases from black culture, Marx, and the psychedelic movement. Marijuana was as common as cigarettes; a faculty–student party welcoming a philosopher featured a rock-and-roll band. (Campus police who were being coopted by the FBI came by to check us out.) I developed a course in group dynamics—a free-wheeling, experiential, self-reflective, pot-boiler rendition of a course I had taught with Freed Bales at Harvard; it became so popular that Mary was hired to teach an additional section. A national guide to campuses described the course as one of the major educational events at Swarthmore. Now as I think back on some of the exercises we engaged in I shiver with amazement and some trepidation. On one moonlight evening I recall a session outside the psychology building, in an apple tree, with each of us, shrouded in pick blossoms, occupying separate limbs. And then there was a class in which the student leaders had us all doing experiential exercises in the college pool—naked in the dark. Psychology became one of the most popular majors at the school.

Our work in the field, and now on the antiwar movement, on drugs, and political activism also meant further changes in my views of psychological science. The field that had once excited me because of its promise of precise, empirically grounded principles of broad generality and enormous utility for society was becoming more suspect. Psychology's claims to political neutrality seemed dangerously naïve, experimental methods seemed increasingly manipulative and intrusive, laboratory findings seemed increasingly artificial and irrelevant to common life, and the theoretical claims increasingly limited to particular historical and cultural circumstances. I presented some of my views at the meetings of the Society for Experimental Social Psychology. John Lanzetta, the editor of the central journal of the field, *The Journal of Personality and Social Psychology*, was worried about the creeping conventionality of the field and asked if he could publish the piece. Although he had difficulties locating anyone to review the manuscript, he published "Social Psychology as History" as the last paper in a 1972 issue. I was totally unprepared for the shock waves that were to follow. Some were enthralled with the fresh air of reflective critique, but more were outraged . . . What came to be known as the "crisis in social psychology" was on . . .

Dog Days

We had moved to a new house, a sprawling three-story stone structure nestled in the woods near the campus. While it had "wonderful potential," it exacted an enormous price in time and resources to peel back the layers of decrepitude and to locate the once elegant landscaping under choking vines. Soon after acquiring the house, we also acquired a foster daughter, Erika, whose parents had been tragically taken from her. We now had from zero to five children between us, depending on the vantage point.

As the house was finished and the children began to leave home, we seemed to be gaining on our challenges. In 1984, after receiving her PhD in psychology at Temple University, Mary began her tenure track job in psychology and Women's Studies at Brandywine, a local campus of Penn State; it was an ideal place for combining her various professional interests. Difficulties began, however, when after a wonderful ski holiday in Wengen, Switzerland, Ken remained to give lectures at the Graduate School of Business in St. Gallen. Perhaps we should have seen the handwriting on the wall. It was the coldest winter in both Switzerland and Philadelphia in a hundred years. Life was miserable apart. Ken was put up with an 85-year-old landlady, Frau Fherlien, who proved to be the single oasis of warmth and comfort. In April, Mary, who had taken on the challenge of developing funds and speakers for a large conference at Penn State, produced the faculty colloquium. It was a gratifying event, gathering together a wide variety of speakers, who spoke about the ways that feminism had influenced their professional disciplines. These talks became the basis of her first book, *Feminist Thought and the Structure of Knowledge* (1988). At the conclusion of the conference, however, she felt drained, empty, and depressed, and she cried over nothing but the relief of nine months of stress. At home, Ken and John Shotter lifted her spirits with champagne.

Thirteen months later, the shattering news: Mary is suffering from cancer, and requires immediate surgery.

Moments from the "cancer ward": The terror is shared. It is happening to us. Who is suffering more? It is not clear. Do we have a chance, do we have a future? Again the grim ambiguity. We are together in hospital rooms; we join in a fog of anesthetic; we sit together watching Wimbledon on the hospital bed; we eat wonderful pâtés and drink white wine smuggled in to celebrate a completed operation. Our friends, especially Bobbie and Gudmund Iversen, Maggie Skitarelic, and the Stroebe's are enormously supportive; many others join in to prevent the bastard from grinding us down. The operations are effective, and six weeks later Ken arranges a week's vacation trip to London. But the possibility of microscopic cells lingering is ever present, and Mary cannot evade chemotherapy. On the Wednesdays of her sessions, he arrives at the door of the purgatory room with a rose. On each session a new rose, and counting. Her hairless, scar-torn body is now battered with the curing poisons. It tears at his insides to hear the wretching. At midnight it ends, and she curls around him, making a connection so that her head and arm enclose him, and her leg touches his, making a circuit of healing energy that floods her body. On Fridays she returns to a day of teaching. She never misses a day of class. The following summer, with a clean bill of health, we celebrate with a summer of revenge in Europe.

Professional life also continued, but the terrain became ever more treacherous. Intellectual adventures were easier in the smaller enclaves of discontent; here it was possible to find a keen appreciation for the various lurchings toward social constructionism, feminist standpoints, historical understanding, and reflexive critique. However, as this work began to surface—as its implications drew notice in the more established wings of the professions—the savagery began. Especially Ken was pilloried: in a draft of a chapter for the *Handbook of Social Psychology* his mentor, E.E. Jones, likened him to a dog barking in the night; as Ken addressed an Oxford conference, his undergraduate professor at Yale, Bob Abelson, took out his newspaper and began to read, a spiteful reaction to the talk; at an Alpach seminar, Karl Popper publicly addressed him as "the enemy"; and at conference in Gerona, Spain, philosopher John Searle spontaneously leaped to the stage after Ken's address and loudly lashed out for a quarter of an hour. But then again, perhaps the donkey kicks hardest when the thorns are most piercing. Fortunately, we were also blessed by the close and supportive friendship of colleagues: John Shotter, Jill Morawski, Anne Marie and John Rijsman, and many others . . .

An Almost Perfect Day: September 20, 1991.
A Diary Entry Written at its Close

The weather is "San Francisco"—sunny, cool and promising optimistic events. It is a godsend Saturday: no compelling deadlines, guests, appointments, or dire needs. We are at leisure. But this does not mean sleeping in. Ken never learned the pleasures. He is thus up at a reasonable 8:15 a.m. and makes his way with Jacques, our black lab wannabe, to the kitchen. Later they return to bed to rouse Mary with a tray and newspapers. Because of Ken's Friday trip to the farmer's market, we are treated to fresh orange juice, green zucchini bread, and a rosy pear. Ken adjourns to his study after breakfast to work on a book manuscript due at the publisher in several weeks. After a more thorough look at the papers, Mary clears the dishes and makes a soup. As she finally reaches her study, she is distracted by the sounds of Nana Mouskouri—romantic Greek/French music coming from Ken's study. The music is turned up for his morning shave. Mary can't resist the scene, and joins him for a hug and a snootful of morning air flowing through his open window.

After lunch, we make a date for later afternoon, and return to our computers and the Metropolitan Opera—a dynamic duo. Two hours pass and we slip away from our cerebral companions for an assignation. Jacques waits patiently, then he leaps onto the bed to share whatever tenderness he can.

But the day still retains its beauty, so we locate another excuse to be outdoors. This time it's tennis. At the high-school courts we drill, play tricks on each other, and indulge in point-free games, enjoying the movement without stress. (A totally different tennis from our miserable mixed doubles on Sundays.) We have decided to go to the college for a concert, and we are running late. Quickly we shower, cook, dress, and feed Jacques and Lynx, our old tomcat. Finding ourselves left with only eight minutes to eat, we tell ourselves, "Calm down, for eight minutes we can be completely relaxed." The bean soup is tasty with weisswursts and a half bottle of leftover red wine. But Ken complains that his stomach has been rebelling at the eating practices of the past three nights: we must stop this rushing at meals.

With the complaint duly acknowledged we race out the door to the Swarthmore campus five minutes away. Our destination is the Lang Performance Hall where a new opera about the life of Malcolm X is being presented, a contribution to the multicultural emphasis that Al Bloom has brought with him to the college presidency. Embarrassingly informal in our dress, we exchange greetings with Al and Peggi and others collected there in their formal attire. The performance is very special—a postmodern pastiche of themes and rhythms from myriad cultural climes. It is too special to stay until the end. Afterwards we return to our studies for a short time while the Jacuzzi heats up. The night air is crisply cool and adorned by a full moon. We cannot be indifferent—either to this or to the fortunes of the day we have experienced . . .

Me: It's really difficult to imagine who would appreciate reading all this stuff, especially this last bit. That is surely the most superficial account in the whole chapter—a description of no substance at all.

You: But when you raise this question you seem to presume a stern and critical reader (perhaps a father?). Why do you think your reader isn't interested in who we are, in those trivial details that make us persons instead of personae? And what is this about superficiality? Doesn't this presume that something profound lies behind, inside, somewhere out of sight—and that properly formed words will reveal what is truly there? What kind of presumption is that for a constructionist?

Me: Now you are forcing me into a binary; if I use the word "superficial," you want to charge me with the presumption that I am committed to some form of oppositional term like "depth." How as feminists can we accept this move? Let's look at it in a poststructural way. I figure many of the readers will be viewing these texts with their scholarly hats on. This being so, they will only find the piece filling if it puts challenging concepts or arguments on the plate. Mere chit-chat about life's ups and downs will just be a crashing bore.

You: I can appreciate what you are saying in a relational sense. There isn't just one story, a fundamental reality that we could capture with a careful account. We could tell a lot of different stories, true enough, and in the present telling it would be collectively solipsistic to disregard the dispositions of those to whom we are relating, namely the reader (or is it our fantasy of a reader, or a fantasy of ourselves reading our own lives?). In any case, we don't want to put people to sleep, or god forbid, cause them to dislike us. But don't you think there is intellectual content in all this, not so fully in the content as in the form?

Me: Well, you know I have to agree. We have already talked about this privately. So I guess this question is a hortatory maneuver to get me to talk publicly about the significance of the form. So, stand by for my little lecture on the four underlying principles of form . . .

You: That little sarcasm isn't like you, it's more like me. So who are you trying to be in that display: you, me, or someone else? But I agree, some of it is pretty obvious, like moving from strong "I" positions at the beginning to a blending of identities as the tales unfold. And there is a slightly subtler narrative embedded here on the undoing of the empiricist commitment, the slow replacement with constructionism, and the place of a dramaturgic constructionism in the very formation of our relationship—a kind of "living constructionism" that proceeded the professional articulation some twenty years later. But I don't think everyone would be so alert to see the themes that were worked out in Ken's extravaganza *The Saturated Self,* for example.

Me: I guess you are right here. That book tried to show how concepts of the person have changed from the romantic to the modernist era, and how they are now being eclipsed by the shift to postmodernism. Our treatment here reflects a similar shift: from a romantic conception of our relationship (two souls discovering each other), to a modernist view (the well-formed machine), to a postmodernist view in which we both disappear into an ever shifting relational matrix, where the difference between the actual and the virtual is erased, and the very idea of a narrative trajectory—a life story—is subverted.

You: Whoa . . . hold on there. I'm still very much here.

Me: But then again, just who are you?

You: You nut, I'm just *me.*

Me: But wait, that's who *I* am . . . I think we have a problem.

Us: Maybe we should go somewhere to talk this over in private. But then again, if all we can do in our tête-à-tête is exchange language from the public coffers, how could we ever be "private"?

5

Collaging Voices

Mary Gergen

In the duography presented in previous chapter our attempt was to play with a biographic form in a way that would ultimately blend the voices of two authors into one. Yet, this form still failed to reveal the many voices that essentially "speak an author" at any given time. In whatever we write, we are drawing from a textual tradition that makes its way into our expressions. The next piece explores this territory. Its performative dimension is first represented by the inclusion of a range of voices that have inspired my work. There is a ribboning of texts, both "my own" (in the sense that they represent a unique intersection of a variety of dialogues), and by many of the authors whose ideas I carry with me from those dialogues. In effect, the form of the work instantiates its premises.

I was particularly fascinated by the possibility that the lack of women in the upper echelons of leadership could reflect a dearth of success narratives. One cannot easily aspire to leadership if there are no motivating stories. This led me to examine biographies of success and to distinguish between Manstories and Womanstories. However, while exploring the gendered character of success stories, I also became disenchanted with the very idea of conceptualizing one's life in terms of well-formed narratives. The Womanstories of success seemed non-linear and fragmented, as opposed to the singular, goal-oriented character of Manstories. Also, the fragments of the former seemed to represent relational bonding; the coherent and goal-oriented narrative appeared as a sign of social disconnection. I thus decided to augment the performative nature of the essay that follows by disrupting its own narrative flow, or enabling the form of the piece to carry an antinarrative voice. Thus, the ribboning of voices also serves as a continuous distraction from the narrative telos of the essay. My hope was to meander or sidestep from one stone to another, not coming to a singular point, but rather creating a collage of related meanings. Not only did this seem closer to my life, but perhaps it also represents a more feminine form of telling.

LIFE STORIES: PIECES OF A DREAM

I have heard the mermaids singing, each to each.
—T. S. Eliot (1963, 3)

The songs of mermaids are not like other songs. Mermaids' voices sing beyond the human range—notes not heard, forms not tolerated, and each to each, not one to many, one above all. If we imagine the mermaids, we might almost hear them singing, their voices blending, so that each, in its own special timbre, lends to the harmony of the whole. So it might be as one writes a voice in a choir at the threshold of sensibility. My voice shall be only one of many to be heard.

When you hear one voice, it is the voice of authority, the father's voice, the leader's voice. One voice belongs to an androcentric order. Will our singing mute the single voice before we drown? Or being mermaids, perhaps our burial grave is on the earth, not under the sea?

We need to learn how to see our theorizing projects as . . . "riffing"
between and over the beats of patriarchal theories.
—Sandra Harding (1986a, 649)

This is an interwoven etude about life stories; it seeks to disrupt the usual narrative line, the rules of patriarchal form. Let us escape the culturally contoured modes of discourse. Be free of beginnings and denouements. Yet I too am mired in convention. I am captured by the contours of the commonplace. And danger lurks if I fling myself too far outside the normal curve. It is a conundrum. If I write in all the acceptable ways, I only recapitulate the patriarchal forms. Yet if I violate expectations too grievously, my words become nonsense. Still, the mermaids sing.

Finding voices authentic to women's experience is appallingly difficult. Not
only are the languages and concepts we have . . . male oriented but historically
women's experiences have been interpreted for us by men and male norms.
—Kathryn Rabuzzi (1988, 12)

We play at the shores of understanding. If you assent to the bending of traditional forms, then perhaps our collective act may jostle the sand castles of the ordered kingdom. We need each other, even if we do not always agree.

If we do our work well, "reality" will appear even more unstable,
complex, and disorderly than it does now.
—Jane Flax (1987, 643)

The Paradox of the Private: Our Public Practices

When we tell each other our deepest secrets, we use a public language. The nuances of consciousness, emotions both subtle and profound, inner yearnings, unconscious desires, the whispering of conscience—all of these are created in the matrix of this language. The words form and deform around us as we speak and listen. We swim in a sea of words. Only that which is public can be private. We dwell in a paradox.

Individual consciousness is a socio-ideological fact. If you cannot talk
about an experience, at least to yourself, you did not have it.
—Caryl Emerson (1983, 260)

Our cultures provide models not only for the contents of what we say, but also for the forms by which we say it. We use these forms unwittingly; they create the means by which we interpret our lives. We know ourselves via the mediating forms of our cultures, through telling, and through listening.

What created humanity is narration.
—Pierre Janet (1928, 42)

"Know thyself," a seemingly timeless motto, loses clarity when we hold that our forms of self-understanding are the creation of the unknown multitudes who have gone before us. We have become, we are becoming, because "They" have set out the linguistic forestructures of intelligibility. What then does a personal identity amount to? Who is it that we might know?

Every text is an articulation of the relations between texts, a product of
intertextuality, a weaving together of what has already been produced
elsewhere in discontinuous form; every subject, every author, every self
is the articulation of an intersubjectivity structured within and around
the discourses available to it at any moment in time.
—Michael Sprinker (1980, 325)

If self-understanding is derived from our cultures and the stories we can tell about ourselves are prototypically performed, what implications does this have for our life affairs? The reverberations of this question will ring in our ears.

Every version of an "other" . . . is also the construction of a "self."
—James Clifford (1986, 23)

And, I add, "Every version of a self must be a construction of the other."

Our first mark of identity is by gender. We are called "boy" or "girl" in our first moment of life. Our personal identities are always genderized, so life stories must begin with this. I am concerned with the gendered nature of our life stories. What are Manstories and Womanstories? How do they differ? And what difference do these differences make?

> *The literary construction of gender is always artificial. . . . One can never unveil the "essence" of masculinity or femininity. Instead, all one exposes are other representations.*
> —Linda Kauffman (1986, 314)

This overture suggests the major themes. Countertones may resist articulation. You may not find what you want. The voices mingle and collide. Only in the confluence will the totality be fixed . . . temporarily.

Defining Powers: Doubts about the Structure

What do I mean by the narratives or stories of our lives? When we began our work on the narrative, Kenneth Gergen and I described the traditional narrative as composed of a valued end point; events relevant to this end point; the temporal ordering of these events toward the end point; and casual linkages between events (K.J. Gergen and M.M. Gergen 1983, 1988; M. M. Gergen and K. J. Gergen 1984).

Now I become uneasy. I wonder why this definition must be as it is. Doesn't a definition defend an order of discourse, an order of life? Whose lives are advantaged by this form, and whose disadvantaged? Should we ask?

What are the forms of our life stories? We recognize them as a comedy, a tragedy, a romance, a satire. We know them as they are told. Their plots are implicated in their structures. A climax is a matter of form as well as content. Though separating form and content may be desirable from an analytic point of view, it is also arbitrary. (What are the forms of a Womanstory and a Manstory? How do they differ?)

> *The dramatic structure of conversion . . . where the self is presented as the stage for a battle of opposing forces and where a climactic victory for one force, spirit defeating flesh, completes the drama of the self, simply does not accord with the deepest realities of women's experience and so is inappropriate as a model for women's life writing.*
> —Mary G. Mason (1980, 210)

Should we question the ways in which patriarchal authority has controlled the narrative forms? We would be in good company. Many feminist literary critics have expanded this perspective (see Benstock 1988; DuPlessis 1985; Smith 1987). Writers such as Virginia Woolf (1957) have also struggled with how male domination in literary forms has made some works great and others trivial, some worthy and some not. What has been judged by the authority figures as correct has been granted publication, critical acclaim, and respect; the rest has often been ignored or abused.

> *Both in life and in art, the values of a woman are not the values of a man. Thus, when a woman comes to write a novel, she will find that she is perpetually wishing to alter the established values to make serious what appears insignificant to a man and trivial what is to him important.*
> —Virginia Woolf (1958, 81)

Although androcentric control over literary forms is a serious matter, how much graver is the accusation that the forms of our personal narratives are also under such control? The relationship between one and the other is strong, but the more pervasive nature and consequences of male-dominated life stories are certainly more threatening, at least to me.

> *Narrative in the most general terms is a version of, or a special expression of, ideology: representations by which we construct and accept values and institutions.*
> —Rachel DuPlessis (1985, x)

I would add, "by which we construct and accept ourselves!"

Thus, I become increasingly skeptical of our classical definitions of the narrative. Judgments of what constitutes a proper telling are suspect because what seem to be simple canons of good judgment, aesthetic taste, or even familiar custom may also be unquestioned expressions of patriarchal power. Under the seemingly innocent guise of telling a true story, one's life narrative validates the status quo.

Genderizing: Tenderizing the Monomyth

Myths have carried the form and content of narratives throughout the centuries. They tell us how great events occur, as well as how stories are made. Joseph Campbell (1956), a lover of ancient myths, proposes that there is one fundamental myth, the "monomyth." This myth begins with the hero, who is dedicated to a quest. To accomplish his goal, he ventures forth from the everyday world and goes into the region of the supernatural. Here he encounters strange, dangerous, and powerful forces, which he must vanquish. He struggles mightily and sacrifices much. Upon his eventual success, the victorious hero returns and is rewarded for his great deeds. The monomyth is the hero's myth, and the major Manstory. (I wonder, where is the woman in this story? She is to be found only as a snare, an obstacle, a magic power, or a prize.)

The whole ideology of representational significance is an ideology of power.
—Stephen Tyler (1986, 131)

This monomyth is not just an historical curiosity. It is the basic model for the stories of achievement in everyday lives. Life stories are often about quests; like the monomyth, they are stories of achievement. The story hangs on the end point. Will the goal be achieved or not? In such stories, all is subsumed by the goal. The heroic character must not allow anything to interfere with the quest.

Is a heroine the same as a hero? Some might say that narratives of heroes are equally available to women. I doubt that this is so. Cultural expectations about how the two genders should express their heroism are clearly divergent. Consider the central characters and the major plots of life stories codified in literature, history, or personal narrative; we could easily conclude that women do not belong, at least not in the starring role. The adventures of the hero of the monomyth would make rather strange sense if he were a woman. If he is the subject of the story, she must be the object. In the system, opposites cannot occupy the same position. The hero is the knower. The woman represents the totality of what is to be known. She is life; he is the master of life. He is the main character; she is a supporting actress. He is the actor; she is the acted upon.

Although theoretically the hero was meant generically to stand for individuals of both sexes, actually, like so called "generic man," the hero is a thoroughly androcentric construction.
—Kathryn Rabuzzi (1988, 10)

In general, the cultural repertoire of heroic stories requires different qualities for each gender. The contrast of the ideal narrative line contrasts the autonomous, ego-enhancing hero, single-handedly and single-heartedly progressing toward a goal, with the long-suffering, selfless, socially embedded heroine being moved in many directions, lacking the tenacious focus demanded of a quest.

Culture is male; our literary myths are for heroes, not heroines.
—Joanna Russ (1972, 18)

The differences in our stories are not generally recognized in our culture. In a democratic society, we do not consider the absence of narrative lines as relevant to the unequal representation of people in public positions of power. We do not turn to our biographies to help explain, for example, why we have so few women leading organizations, mountain-climbing expeditions, or math classes (or so few men serving as primary caretakers of children). Even when women are leaders in their professions, or are exceptional in some arena of life, it is difficult for them to tell their personal narratives according to the forms that would be suitable to their male colleagues. They are in a cultural hiatus, with a paucity of stories to tell. (How does one become when no story can be found?)

> *The emphasis by women on the personal, especially on other people, rather than on their work life, their professional success, or their connectedness to current political or intellectual history clearly contradicts the established criterion about the content of autobiography.*
> —Estelle Jelinek (1980, 10)

Feminist Theories and Gender Differences

Various feminist theorists have emphasized the underlying family dynamics that may sustain our gendered stories. As Nancy Chodorow (1978), Dorothy Dinnerstein (1976), Jane Flax (1983), Evelyn Fox Keller (1983), Carol Gilligan (1982), and others have suggested, boys and girls are raised to regard their life trajectories differently. All children have as their first love object their mothering figure. However, boys are reared to separate from their mothers; they learn to replace their attachment to mother with pride in masculine achievements and to derogate women and their relationships with them. Girls are not cut away from their mothers and are forced to continue to identify themselves with them. They remain embedded in their relations and do not learn the solitary hero role. But they must bear the burden of shame that the androcentered culture assigns to their gender. Each man and woman acquires for personal use a repertoire of potential life stories relevant to his or her own gender. Understanding one's past, interpreting one's actions, and evaluating future possibilities—each is filtered through these stories. Events "make sense" as they are placed in the proper story form. If certain story forms are absent, events cannot take on the same meaning as if they were there. We assume that life "produces" the autobiography as an act produces its consequence, but can we not suggest, with equal justice, that "the autobiography project may itself produce and determine life" (de Man 1979, 920)?

Autobiographies as Gendered Stories of Our Lives

I have been studying the popular autobiographies of men and women. Of interest to me is not only what is there, in the story lines, but what is missing as well. What is it that each gender cannot talk about and thus cannot integrate into life stories and life plans? What can a Manstory tell that a Womanstory cannot, and vice versa?

> *What appears as "real" in history, the social sciences, the arts, even in common sense, is always analyzable as a restrictive and expressive set of social codes and conventions.*
> —James Clifford (1986, 10)

In critical works concerning autobiography, women's narratives have been almost totally neglected (see Olney 1980; Sayre 1980; Smith 1974). Women's writings have usually been exempted because they did not fit the proper formal mold (Lieblich, Tuval-Mashiach, and Zilber 1998). Their work has been more fragmentary, multidimensional, understated, and temporally disjunctive. "Insignificant" has been the predominant critical judgment toward women's autobiographies (and their lives) (Jelinek 1980).

> When a woman writes or speaks herself into existence, she is forced
> to speak in something like a foreign tongue.
> —Carolyn Burke (1978, 844)

Interpreting the Stories

> I look into autobiographies to discover the forms we use to tell a Manstory, a Womanstory. What story can I tell? Autobiography reveals the impossibility of its own dream: what begins on the presumption of self-knowledge ends in the creation of a fiction that covers over the premises of its construction.
> —Shari Benstock (1988, 11)

My materials are taken from many autobiographies. This chapter concentrates on just a few. In this way, a sense of life may perhaps be felt. The quotations I have drawn from these texts are hardly proof of my conclusions; they are better viewed as illustrations to vivify my interpretations. Other interpretations can and should be made by me and by others.

The Quest: traditional narratives demand an end point, a goal. Concentrating on the goal, moving toward the point, putting events in a sequence, building the case (no tangents, please)—these rhetorical moves are required by custom. Classical autobiographies delineate the life of cultural heroes, those who have achieved greatness through their accomplishments. We expect that those who write their biographies will be such heroes.

> Men tend to idealize their lives or to cast them into heroic
> molds to project their universal import.
> —Estelle Jelinek (1980, 14)

How single-minded are those heroes in pursuit of their goals? How committed are the women who write their biographies? Do their stories also fit the classic mold? Listen to some of their voices. Lee Iacocca's best-selling autobiography (1984) focuses on his automotive career. His family life, in contrast, receives scant attention. Iacocca's wife, Mary, was a diabetic. Her condition worsened over the years; after two heart attacks, one in 1978 and the other in 1980, she died, in 1983, at the age of fifty-seven. According to Iacocca, each of the heart attacks came following a crisis period in his career at Ford or at Chrysler. Iacocca writes, "Above all, a person with diabetes has to avoid stress. Unfortunately, with the path I had

chosen to follow, this was virtually impossible" (1984, 301). Obviously, his description of his wife's death is not intended to expose his cruelty. It is, I think, a conventional narrative report appropriate to his gender. The book (and his life) are dedicated to his career. It appears that Iacocca would have found it unimaginable that he should have ended or altered his career to improve his wife's health. As a Manstory, the passage is not condemning; however, read in reverse, as a wife's description of the death of her husband or child, it would appear callous, to say the least. A woman who would do such a thing would not be considered an outstanding folk hero, as Iacocca has been for many people. She might instead be scorned or worse.

Yeager is the autobiography of the quintessential American hero, the pilot with the "right stuff." Yeager's story is intensively focused on his career in the Air Force. His four children, born in quick succession, provided a highly stressful challenge for his wife, who became gravely ill during her last pregnancy. Nothing stopped him from flying, however. Constantly moving around the globe, always seeking out the most dangerous missions, he openly states, "Whenever Glennis needed me over the years, I was usually off in the wild blue yonder" (Yeager and Janos 1985, 103). America's favorite hero would be considered an abusive parent were his story regendered.

Richard Feynman, autobiographer and Nobel prize-winning physicist, was married to a woman who had been stricken with tuberculosis for seven years. During the war years, he moved out to Los Alamos to work on the Manhattan Project (developing the atomic bomb), while she was several hours away in a hospital in Albuquerque. The day she was dying, he borrowed a car to go to her bedside. He reports: "When I got back (yet another tire went flat on the way), they asked me what happened. 'She's dead. And how's the program going?' They caught on right away that I didn't want to moon over it" (1986, 113).

Manstories tend to follow the traditional narrative pattern: men becoming their own heroes, facing crises, following their quests, and ultimately achieving victory. Their careers provide their central lines of narrative structuring, while personal commitments, external to their careers, are relegated to insignificant subplots.

What does one find among women authors?

> *There is virtually only one occupation for a female protagonist—love, of course—which our culture uses to absorb all possible "Bildung," success/failure, learning, education, and transition to adulthood.*
> —Rachel DuPlessis (1985, 182)

Beverly Sills, who became a star performer at the New York City Opera, gave up her singing career for two years to live in Cleveland because this was where her husband had his job. She describes her thoughts:

Peter had spent all of his professional life working for the *Plain Dealer*, and he had every intention of eventually becoming the newspaper's editor-in-chief. I was just going to have to get used to Cleveland. My only alternative was to ask Peter to scuttle the goal he'd been working toward for almost twenty-five years. If I did that, I didn't deserve to be his wife. Not coincidentally, I began reevaluating whether or not I truly wanted a career as an opera singer. I decided I didn't . . . I was twenty-eight years old, and I wanted to have a baby. (Sills and Linderman 1987, 120)

The only businesswoman in my sample, Sydney Biddle Barrows, also known by her autobiography's title, the *Mayflower Madam* (1987), has second thoughts about maintaining a then extremely successful business when it clashes with private goals:

By early 1984 . . . I realized that I couldn't spend the rest of my life in the escort business. I was now in my early thirties and starting to think more practically about my future which would, I hoped, include marriage. As much as I loved my job, I had to acknowledge that the kind of man I was likely to fall in love with would never marry the owner of an escort service . . . If I didn't want to remain single forever, I would sooner or later have to return to a more conventional line of work. (1987, 205)

Martina Navratilova discusses her feelings about going skiing after many years of forgoing this dangerous sport:

I made a decision in my teens to not risk my tennis career on the slopes, but in recent years I've wanted to feel the wind on my face again . . . I wasn't willing to wait God knows how many years to stop playing and start living. (1985, 320)

Nien Cheng's *Life and Death in Shanghai* (1986) details her survival during years of imprisonment in China. Though her own survival might be seen as the major goal of her story, this focus is deeply compromised by her concerns with her daughter's welfare:

I hoped my removal to the detention house would free her from any further pressure to denounce me. If that were indeed the case . . . I would be prepared to put up with anything. (1986, 132)

Discovering that her daughter is dead greatly disturbs her own will to go on:

Now there was nothing left. It would have been less painful if I had died in prison and never known that Meiping was dead. My struggle to keep alive . . . suddenly seemed meaningless. (ibid., 360)

For these women, the career line is important, but it is not an ultimate end point. Whereas the men seem to sacrifice their lives to their careers, the women seem to tell the story in reverse. This is not to say that women avoid

the achievement of goals. They too yearn for the joy of success. But men and women do not describe their feelings in the same way. Let us listen.

Lee Iacocca:

> My years as general manager of the Ford Division were the happiest period of my life. For my colleagues and me, this was fire in the belly time. We were high from smoking our own brand—a combination of hard work and big dreams. (1984, 65)

Chuck Yeager:

> I don't recommend going to war as a way of testing character, but by the time our tour ended we felt damned good about ourselves and what we had accomplished. Whatever the future held, we knew our skills as pilots, our ability to handle stress and danger, and our reliability in tight spots. It was the difference between thinking you're pretty good, and proving it. (Yeager and Janos 1985, 88)

Edward Koch:

> I am the mayor of a city that has more Jews than live in Jerusalem, more Italians than live in Rome . . . and more Puerto Ricans than live in San Juan . . . It is a tremendous responsibility, but there is no other job in the world that compares with it . . . Every day has the possibility of accomplishing some major success. (1984, 359)

When John Paul Getty drilled his first great oil well, he was overjoyed:

> The sense of elation and triumph was and is always there. It stems from knowing that one has beaten nature's incalculable odds by finding and capturing a most elusive (and often a dangerous and malevolent) prey. (1986, 28)

The tone of the male voices often has an element of hostility, aggression, or domination in it. Their celebration of achievement seems to be the result of what is fundamentally an antagonistic encounter between themselves and other people or nature itself. The ways that women's voices speak of achievements take a rather different tone.

Martina Navratilova:

> For the first time I was a Wimbledon champion, fulfilling the dream of my father many years before . . . I could feel Chris [Evert] patting me on the back, smiling and congratulating me. Four days later, the Women's Tennis Association computer ranked me Number 1 in the world, breaking Chris's four-year domination. I felt I was on top of the world. (1985, 190)

Beverly Sills:

> I think "Se Pieta" was the single more extraordinary piece of singing I ever did. I know I had never heard myself sing that way before . . . The curtain began coming down very slowly . . . and then a roar went

through that house the likes of which I'd never heard. I was a little stunned by it: the audience wouldn't stop applauding. (Sills and Linderman 1987, 172)

Sydney Biddle Barrows:

I was motivated by the challenge of doing something better than everyone else . . . I was determined to create a business that would appeal to . . . men, who constituted the high end of the market . . . I was sure that we could turn our agency into one hell of an operation—successful, elegant, honest, and fun. (1987, 48–49)

In the Womanstories, the love of the audience response, the affection of the opponent, and the satisfaction of customers are the significant factors. The achievement is described in relational terms, with more stress on mutuality than supremacy. The Womanstory emphasizes continuity with the goals of others, not opposition to them. In fact, it is possible for one's opponent to be seen as a necessary part of one's own success. As Martina Navratilova says:

You're totally out for yourself, to win a match, yet you're dependent on your opponent to some degree for the type of match it is and how well you play. You need the opponent; without her you do not exist. (1985, 162)

Emotional Interdependence

What do these stories tell about emotional interdependency—that is, the desire to be with others and to engage in reciprocal affection? Here, the Manstories appear to be rather thin. Sticking to the narrative line may cut short men's affective lives, at least in print. But this is too black and white a message. Men have their buddies, sidekicks, intimate rivals, and compatriots. Perhaps the difference is that together they look outward, rather than at each other. Let us look at how Manstories allow for the expression of relatedness and emotionality.

Ed Koch, reporting a conversation:

I've been Mayor for close to three years . . . I get involved in a lot of controversies and I make a lot of people mad at me, and so maybe at the end of these four years they'll say, "He's too controversial and we don't want him!" And maybe they'll throw me out. That's okay with me. I'll get a better job, and you won't get a better mayor. (1984, 227)

Chuck Yeager:

Often at the end of a hard day, the choice was going home to a wife who really didn't understand what you were talking about . . . or gathering around the bar with guys who had also spent the day in a cockpit. Talking flying was the next best thing to flying itself. And after

we had a few drinks in us, we'd get happy or belligerent and raise some hell. Flying and hell raising—one fueled the other. (Yeager and Janos 1985, 173)

John Paul Getty's diaries might serve to provide insight into a father's true feeling about his sons:

> For some reason, I have always been much freer in recording my emotions and feelings in my diaries . . .
>
> *1939 Los Angeles, California, May 20*: Saw George, a remarkable boy, rapidly becoming a man. He is 5'9" tall and weighs 145 pounds.
>
> *Geneva, Switzerland, July 8*: Ronny is well, happy and likes his school. His teachers give him good report. He is intelligent and has good character, they say. Took Ronny and Fini to the Bergues Hotel for lunch and then to Chamonix.
>
> *Los Angeles, December 10*: Went to Ann's house [Ann Rork, my fourth wife, who divorced me in 1935] and saw Pabby and Gordon, bless them. They are both fine boys. (1986, 11)

Manstories seem to celebrate the song of the self. Emotional ties are mentioned as "facts" where necessary, but the author does not try to recreate in the reader empathic emotional responses. Getty's descriptions of his interactions with his sons, for example, are very meager in emotional feelings, despite his claim that the diary entries show his depth of caring. The willingness to play the role of the "bastard" is also seen in Manstories, as, for example, in Koch's remarks above.

What about our heroines? What do their stories tell about their emotional interdependencies? How important are relationships to their life courses? Is there a Womanstory, too?

Let us listen: Beverly Sills reminisces that "one of the things I always loved best about being an opera singer was the chance to make new friends every time I went into a new production" (Sills and Linderman 1987, 229). She writes that when she and Carol Burnett were doing a television show together, they cried when the show was over: "We knew we'd have nobody to play with the next day. After that we telephoned each other three times a day" (ibid., 280).

Martina Navratilova writes that "I've never been able to treat my opponent as the enemy, particularly Pam Shriver, my doubles partner and one of my best friends" (1985, 167).

Sydney Biddle Barrows (1987) emphasizes in her book her ladylike upbringing, her sensitive manners, and her appreciation of the finer things of life. Her lifestyle is obviously besmirched when she is arrested by the police and thrown in jail. She writes about leaving a group of streetwalking prostitutes with whom she has been jailed: "As I left the cell, everybody started shouting and cheering me on. 'Go get 'em, girlfren?' I left with mixed emotions. These girls had been so nice to me, and so open and interesting, that my brief experience in jail was far more positive than I could have imagined" (1987, 284).

The necessity of relating to others that is observable in Womanstories is especially crucial in Nien Cheng's narrative about solitary confinement. To contend with the long and bitter loneliness, she adopted a small spider as a friend. She describes her concern for this spider:

> My small friend seemed rather weak. It stumbled and stopped every few steps. Could a spider get sick, or was it merely cold? . . . It made a tiny web on the toilet edge . . . forming something rather like a cocoon . . . When I had to use the toilet, I carefully sat well to one side so that I did not disturb it. (1986, 155)

These examples, though limited, illustrate the major differences I have found between the relatively more profound emotional interdependency and intimacy requirements of women's narratives as opposed to those of men. In general, the important aspects of women's autobiographies depend heavily on their affiliative relationships with others. They seem to focus on these ties without drawing strong demarcations between their work world and their "private" life. Their stories highlight the interdependent nature of their involvements much more vividly than do the stories of the men. The centrality of emotional well-being to all facets of life is found there much more frequently than in the men's stories.

Voices as Verses: Forms and Foam

As stories are told, forms are recreated. The content belongs to the forms, and the forms control the content. Let us look at the forms more closely.

> *Individuals have characteristic ways of navigating their lives. What is characteristic, the signature we read across episodes, exists at the level of narrative structure. We can analyze the structure of a life plot as symbolic in its own right.*
> —Richard Ochberg (1988, 172)

Popular autobiographies of men are very similar in form. Their narrative lines tend to be linear (that is, strongly related to an explicit goal state, the career or quest) and progressive (the action moves toward this goal). Manstories also tend to be characterized by one or two major climaxes, usually related to career trajectories. The emphasis men place on the single narrative line is evident from the very beginning of their book. Edward Koch's autobiography *Mayor*, for example, is totally devoted to his political career, especially as it "mirrors" the life of New York City. Chapter 1, entitled "A Child of the City," begins not with a biological childhood but with his political youth: "In March of 1975, when I was a U.S. Congressman from New York . . ." Koch begins at a crisis point for the book's long-suffering heroine—not a flesh-and-blood woman, but New York City. Chuck Yeager's book about his life as a pilot begins with a crash landing. Getty opens his book with a sentence indicating that he was born in 1892 and has been "an active businessman since 1914" (1986, vii). Physicist Feynman starts with, "When I was about eleven or twelve I set up a lab in my house" (1986, 3). Iacocca states, "You're about to read the history of a man who's had more than his share of successes" (1984, xiv). The origin of the life story is at the beginning of one's professional career.

> *The autobiographer confronts personally her culture's stories of male and female desire, insinuating the lines of her story through the lines of the patriarchal story that has been autobiography.*
> —Sidonie Smith (1987, 19)

Womanstories also contain a progressive theme related to achievement goals, but often the text emphasizes another facet of personal identity and deviates from one clear narrative line associated with career. Beverly Sills' first chapter recalls the last night she sang at the New York City opera house at a gala charity performance. The event is presented not as a career triumph, but rather as an emotionally significant "swan song" (Sills and Linderman 1987). Sydney Biddle Barrows' book (1987) commences with a description of the annual meeting of the Society of Mayflower Descendants of which she is a member, thus foregrounding the question of how, as a member of such an elitist social group, she became the owner of an escort service. Nien Cheng (1986) recalls her old home in Shanghai, her daughter asleep in her room. The importance of her daughter's activities plays a strong counterpoint to her own existential issues. "Apple Trees" is the title of Martina Navratilova's first chapter; she begins, "I was three years old when my mother and father divorced" (1985, 1). For female authors, the story forms available are much fuller (and more multiple in perspective) than for the men. Career successes and failures are mingled with other issues of great personal importance. Thus, the story line becomes less clearly demarcated, the narrative threads are more complexly woven. A woman's story is about a person who is embedded in a variety of relationships, all of which have some priority in the telling of her life. Ambiguities about any outcome make more complex the task of giving value to any particular event.

Can Stories/Lives Be Changed?

Throughout this chapter, I have illustrated how personal identities are construed through gendered life stories. Autobiographies exemplify the repertoire of life story forms by which "significant" members of a culture define themselves. Less important people, those who merely tell their stories to themselves and their private audiences, also use these forms. We all know ourselves, define our pasts, and project our futures as they fit into the acculturated story forms. But the forms for each gender are restrictive, and in many critical areas, such as achievement strivings and intimate relationships, men and women are inhibited from formulating selves that would allow for a different range of expressions and actions. Neither a man nor a woman can easily swap roles without the loss of social approval.

> *The structure of autobiography, a story that is at once by and about the same individual, echoes and reinforces a structure already implicit in our language, a structure that is also (not accidentally) very like what we usually take to be the structure of self-consciousness itself: the capacity to know and simultaneously be that which one knows.*
> —Elizabeth W. Bruss (1980, 301)

I began this work with a special sensitivity to the losses that women have endured because of their absence from the public sphere. I saw that because the story lines that lead a woman from childhood to maturity did not show the path by which strong achievement strivings could be satisfied without great personal sacrifice: women could not become all they had the potential to be. As I read the autobiographies of our "great" men, I confronted anew what many social critics, especially feminists, have frequently claimed: that the goals, values, and methods that sustain men's lives are antagonistic to other significant social values, those associated with women's narratives and lives. In revising these stories, I saw the basic values of each clustering congregate around themes of power versus themes of love. Increasingly, as I read, it seemed to me that what most needed change was not women's narratives, to become more like men's, but the reverse. Men, perhaps even more than women, needed new story lines, lines that were more multiplex, relational, and "messy." Both men and women seemed imprisoned by their stories; both bound to separate pieces of the world that, if somehow put together, would create new possibilities in which each could share the other's dreams. But how can we escape our story lines, our prisons made of words?

> *Plots are dramatic embodiments of what a culture believes to be true . . . Of all the possible actions people can do in fiction, very few can be done by women.*
> —Joanna Russ (1972, 4)

Language: Source and Sorceress

Language seems almost magical. Only through its powers to name can we identify our experiences and our persons. There are no social structures that bear upon us beyond this linguistic order. All that exists is within it. If we want to change our lives, we need to change our patterns of discourse. The "language games" constitute what there is to change. Can we lift ourselves by our bootstraps?

> *Individuals construct themselves as subjects through language, but individual subjects rather than being the source of their own self-generated and self-expressive meaning adopt positions available within the language at a given moment.*
> —Felicity Nussbaum (1988, 149)

Our narrative forms, our metaphors, our ways of communicating do not emerge from nothingness. They are embedded in the foundations of society. Stories and their structural instantiations reverberate against and with each other. Are we prisoners of our father tongue? Yes—mostly—maybe—sometimes—no. Perhaps we can, at least, wiggle a bit.

> *In altering the images and narrative structures through which we compose the stories of our lives, we may hope to alter the very experiences of those lives as well.*
> —Annette Kolodny (1980, 258)

Many voices singing different tunes can sound noisy. Do you feel drowned out? We must sing like mermaids and hope that a melody or two will be carried on the wind.

> *Subversively, she rearranges the dominant discourse and the dominant ideology of gender, seizing the language and its power to turn cultural fictions into her very own story.*
> —Sidonie Smith (1987, 175)

How do we rearrange the melodies of talk? I will suggest some ways. Let us listen carefully as our words divide us and emphasize power differences among us. Let us resist these discordant tunes. (This will be less appealing at first to those whose words have been on everyone's lips.) Let us note, for example, that we call ourselves for some man long since dead. In a sense we belong to him. Let our names hang lightly in the air, or let us blow them away if we wish.

> *For a symbolic order that equates the idea(l) of the author with a phallic pen transmitted from father to son places the female writer in contradiction to the dominant definition of woman and casts her as the usurper of male prerogatives.*
> —Domna Stanton (1984, 13)

Let us listen to the metaphors we carry with us. Let us choose them carefully. Do we mimic our brothers who scoff at "soft" sciences and who love "hard" data? Do we feel the grasp of "sexual politics" at our throats?

> *To change a story signals a dissent from social norms as well*
> *as narrative forms.*
> —Rachel DuPlessis (1985, 20)

Let us play with story lines. Let us not always conform to androcentric styles. Let us demur. Maybe stories don't need lines. Perhaps they need to step out of the queue and refuse to march in orderly progression. Let us not stick to the point. Let us improvise!

> *The construction is nothing more than an improvisation.*
> —George Rosenwald (1988, 256)

Let us claim the tentative and fuzzy nature of all our linguistic formulations. Let us shake the tree of knowledge, unashamed. Let us eat the apple to the core, and spit out "truth." Let us grant ourselves the pleasures of making languages, and changing them, as they transform us. Let us sing songs that will free us from the past and hum sweet dirges for androcentric systems as they drown.

6

Multiplying Metaphors

Mary Gergen

This essay was designed to explore the potentials of combining social constructionist theory with a feminist perspective in gender studies. The challenge is not an insignificant one, as the essentialism of feminist ideology, along with a realist view of gender and social structure, generate a resistance to the nonfoundationalist stance of constructionism, and its associated vision of multiple realities. At the same time, however, many constructionists—including the post-structuralist and postmodern scholars from the humanities—have strong investments in feminist politics and values. I include my own work in this camp. How, then, can the two orientations be reconciled? And more importantly, what does feminism gain by "going postmodern"?

In writing this piece, my postmodern constructionist stance gave me the freedom to break with the traditional academic writing style and move with more passion and rhetorical freedom. In particular, I allowed myself to explore the potentials of multiple metaphors. At the outset, this essay was inspired by an image of a pebble skipping over a pond. Each time the pebble strikes the water, a new set of ripples is set in motion. As the ripples spread, collide, and combine, the entire surface of the pond is set in motion. Here again we subvert what I view as a more masculine orientation to writing—straight ahead and to the point. Why impoverish the world through such systematics? Why not recognize the multiplicities and their intersections, and allow their combinations to fill spaces of understanding? This form disturbs the tranquility of the seemingly straightforward path that foundationalist arguments take. The waters of certainty are roiled.

One might say that the moments in which the stone strikes the water are also entries into new and differing metaphoric worlds. There are stop signs, and caravans, and fairy tales, and more. There is a further element of performativity represented in the wordplay. The word play disrupts the kind of instrumental reading habit that simply searches for the point and disregards the rest. Further, by injecting moments of playfulness into writing, the truth-bearing character of the text is undermined. The reader is at once asked to take the text seriously but not as a final philosophy. I also like forms of wordplay that encourage the reader to process the sentences orally. Such oral engagement enables the reader to "feel the text" from the inside.

SKIPPING STONES: CIRCLES IN THE POND

> *Every . . . text is the absorption and transformation of other texts.*
> —Julia Kristeva (1998, 28)

The flow of discourse swirls among us. How do we enter the stream? Some profess that knowledge flows from pitchers into cups, conveyed from one server to the next. Others say it travels in circles, simultaneously, mutually, reverberating sensations of sound and motion to create more than one experience. Some say it is a symphony of sound, others say it's a damn racket!

This text is as a skipping stone, flung along a pond, and as it skips and sinks, it makes circles that ripple to the shores. Where do all these ripples go? Meanings fragmented and made whole. Sounds—harmonious and dissident—echo and collide, foam up, and blend into chambers far from home.

The Circles: Intersecting the Social Constructionist Moment with the Feminist Forever

We are intersecting: inter-*sex*-ion . . . a mutabil-ing of differences, sexual and otherwise, a blending, converging, and complexifying—a conundrum of possibilities, losing clear identity and stable purpose in the converging traffic; becoming all together, and going out beyond, where we have not dared to go before. It is a risky business, and pleasure.

Postmodern feminists, circle merging with circle, traveling as one on a Mobius strip, with more twists than a Philadelphia pretzel—an endless turning of possible divines. What future can we share?

It is fast company; our reputations are at risk. French philosophers, Lacanian lounge lizards, Foucaultian for(a)gers, Queer choirs and Straight compatriots, High-theory culties, Lionized leftists, Nightmarching matriarchs, Political polly-technicians—all barreling down the road at outrageous speeds.

Oh, the good ol'days, when we could see forever, high above this motley crew, where "hot air" kept our balloons aloft. Eternity and the world below us. Wasn't that grand? We've had to leave that God trick, as Donna Haraway said, to those who claim a "vision from everywhere and nowhere, equally and fully" (1988, 577). We're just stuck staring through glasses spattered with the mud and minutia of the millennia. Forever's fogged up. The rose-colored glasses have lost their tint.

As a postmodern post-ette, Ellen Rosenau has said: "Postmodernism questions causality, determinism, egalitarianism, humanism, liberal democracy, necessity, objectivity, rationality, responsibility, and truth" (1992, 5). How can a feminist deal with that? What more could one despise, or wish for?

What have these feminists traded for, in this interchange? As modernists, in the limelight, we stood with the beacons of Enlightenment, illuminated in our quest. Our cow ELECTRIC. In this trade we've pulled our own plug, and now embrace the dark—empty, vast, and full of strange sounds.

Some think it's a Jack and the Beanstalk deal: a handful of beans for a living, breathing neon cow. How Now, Brown Cow? What do you have to say for yourself?

And what about this new stairway to the stars? The Constructionist Causeway. We're offered a spiraling, spindly kite tale on which to balance our act, to situate ourselves firmly in midair, on a swinging beanstalk. Is this worth giving up the promises of impartial truth and law, foundational methods, and accumulations of facts? Can we accept, as Jane Flax has declared (1990, 127), that "ultimately nothing justifies our claims, beyond each person's desire and the discursive practices in which these are developed, embedded, and legitimated"?

Yet, some of us are spellbound too. Words bind us in their spell? Starry-eyed, wanting to throw over the dull and straight and narrow paths set down before us, can we not grab for the ring? Brass-filled knuckles—they have a certain grip on us as well.

Let's say yes, but it's a High Anxiety situation. There is much to criticize, and we've all done our share. Craig Owens adds to the drama: "Few women have engaged in the modernism/postmodernism debate . . . [P]ostmodernism may be another masculine invention engineered to exclude women" (1983, 61).

But we could fix that.

The pm framework is so bare . . . skeletons on parade. It is too lean for our tastes. Feminist social constructionists offer some meat for those bones. Something to hang on it . . . but we simply won't be "hangers on."

Do we talk in circles? Is that all we can do? Can we even do that? Enveloped within language communities, our words skittering by one another. Words may sound the same, but can they ever be heard as such? Words swing and sway to new makings in each separate clime.

How do we talk aloud? Can we speak for others? Can others speak for us? What are we saying? Can we keep track? What track can we keep? If we tear up the tracks, can we still find a way?

Pastiche personality Beryl C. Curt has said: "Language which flows naturally and easily must always, in a 'climate of problematization,' arouse suspicion. Its very ease and fluidity helps to beguile the reader into believing the text is merely mirroring the world 'as it really is,' and obscures its ability to glamour that reality into being" (1994, 14).

Turning about, searching for my tale, I plead guilty as well. I wish to glamour a reality into being, spreading glitter, mascara, and rouge, preening these words into worlds. And yet, PAUSE, I am roughing up the language, sandpapering the senses, as well. You may well step with caution.

Trouble can be good. Jane Flax argues: "The single most important advance in feminist theory is that the existence of gender relations has been problematized" (1990, 27). So the conversation continues. But in a world of surging circles, isn't that our salvation? Not everyone agrees.

There's a Stop Sign in the Traffic Circle—someone wants to know if we have a license to practice these words. What happened to practice? We can't sit around all day talking. Things happen, don't they? Talk is cheap, they say. Actions speak louder than words. In a word . . . WHERE HAVE ALL THE POLITICS GONE? Have they vanished? Suspicion looms: how can we sue in the name of justice, on the basis of our sex, when sex is only someone's construction, and justice just a name? How can deconstruction be our friend? With friends like that, who needs enemies? Some whisper, "Even if everything is only socially constructed, why not just keep it our little secret? What good would it be to tell the world." How many of us are closet constructionists? When are we going to have an outing?

Jane Flax, from the backseat: "We need to learn ways of making claims about and acting upon injustice without transcendental guarantees or illusions of innocence" (1993, 141). We agree with Jane. We could give up modernist versions of truth, objectivity, and a single knowable reality. We could learn to love RELATIVITY—perhaps.

All conversation stops when this trick is pulled . . . is she the devil in drag? Horns aplenty or plenty horny. What is to be done with her?

Everybody knows that a "relativist" believes the most outlandish things. Every explanation is as good as another; all things are equal. The moon is made of cheese. The Earth is flat. Man comes from monkeys . . . World War II did not occur. But where, the enemy asks, does the equal sign come from? Smuggled in from the contraband caravan? A Rhetorical Trick . . . Who would survive the toll of that blast?

Reject the sign. Nothing is equal. There are many stories and many contexts: how shall I compare them? . . . Again, many stories and many contexts.

If you didn't have foundations, relativism could not exist. No attack without foundations. Who ever wonders about the costs of a foundationalist metatheory? Why is it evil to doubt one's own worldview? Is it possible that Certainty is the real devil around here? Is not the God's eye view the enemy?

Do we know for sure who was right in Vietnam, Nagasaki, or Berlin? Is it always a good question to ask? How have those in power used Absolute Truth and goodness to tie their nation's youth up in tourniquet knots?

Perhaps we need a new entry into the DSM IV—DAS, Descartes' Anxiety Syndrome. The symptoms include existential angst, fear of chaos, and melancholia for the loss of foundational principles. Are there cures for this dis-ease? Consider Patti Lather's words:

> Relativity has been put forth as the great bugbear against which we must commit to some foundational absolute if anarchy and chaos are not to descend upon us . . . Such claims are cultural dominants which masquerade as natural, rational, necessary, but which are less a fact of nature than of human production. They are, in spite of their denial, embedded in . . . the power/knowledge nexus which provides the constraints and possibilities of discourse. (1991, 117)

Feminists may not jive to relativism, but they do not blanch at uncertainty. We can live without all this security. Foundations have never been much protection to the dis-staffed.

Let's Lighten Up: Get Practical, Move into Circles of Action

Where are the roads taking us?

A new breed of scholars has recently arrived on the scene. Called the Empiricist Social Constructionists, they have evolved by taking "the best" from both worlds. By winnowing the wheat of social constructionist theory from the chaff of the metaphysical, they take social constructionist theory and prove it with data. Here are "thirteen ways of looking at an ESC."

Where do you see your shadow?

All things are socially constructed, except history.
All things are socially constructed, except my emotions and personal experiences.
All social things are social constructions, but "material conditions" are not.

All social things are social constructions, but "spiritual reality" is not.

All societal things are social constructions, but natural things like rocks are not. (Here toe stubbing is mentioned quite often, or sometimes running into walls.)

Gender roles are socially constructed, but biological categories, like males and females, are not.

Concepts are socially constructed, but facts are not.

Everything is socially constructed, but social constructionism is not.

Some things are socially constructed and some things aren't. You don't know until you do an experiment on them.

Scientists using empirical methods can prove whether or not social constructionist theories are true.

There's a grain of truth in the notion, but constructionist just go too far.

Some of my best friends are social constructionists.

I like what I hear, if only I could read that weird stuff.

We cannot stop our journey here. Rather, we must follow the path of the untried and untrue. Entering this new zone, things are a bit strange. Some might say bizarre. Yet, colors on the rim of the world are glowing. They beckon and invite. Let's follow the trail a bit further.

What if we take all the challenges together?

that language is not a transparent representation of the world

that realities are cultural constructions

that polarities do not exist in nature, but in language

that facts are neither true nor false, except by the ordination of the social groups involved

that we must apply values via a leap of faith alone

that political actions are deeds of faith

that identity and knowledge are critically dependent upon interaction to be created, and are partial, fragmented, and temporary

What does this bode for future feminist inquiry? We can:

Critique: de-mystifying old knowledge, destabilizing old systems, undermining foundational assumptions and a priori statements;

Respect: nothing valued from the past must be jettisoned. Not experiments, statistics, or observational designs, as long as we do not mistake their evidence for trails to Truth;

Invent: Possibilities for new conversations, new interchanges, new interpretations, new actions;

Commit: the Big C word finds its resting place again. This time, it's a dangerous enterprise. One commits without the consolations of certainty. One dares commitment; one accepts the risks. If we value equality, or nurturing, or assertiveness, or any other stance, we must stand up and be counted, even as we accept that there are no foundations to defend us, except the willingness of others to share our visions and our dreams.

Play: with the notion of the relational as the core of the enterprise. If we are created and create through engagement in the world around us and within us, then our identities and subjectivities, our values and preferences are linked to these interactions. "I am you" or "I am via you" or "we are, together."

Feminist/social constructionism alters ways of living, working, loving life and each other in the tenor of each day. Diana Whitney describes the social constructionist in the realm of spirituality: "A social construction-ist view claims relatedness as the organizing principle for life . . . This shift implies a movement from the view of spiritual development as a possession of the individual, to a view of spiritual development as a quality of relationship: first, one's relationship with spirit . . . and then with a web of other relationships . . . people, plants, and animals" (1995, 2). Patti Lather: "This issue is not so much where poststructuralism comes from, but what it will be" (1995, 41).

Let's all be there together.

7

The Dialogic Alternative

Mary Gergen, with Kip Jones

One of the most attractive routes to performative writing is dialogue. Although it is challenging to compose dialogue for the theatre or a novel, writing that enacts "oneself" can usually be performed with ease. For many, it is an easier form of writing than the monologic essay, as one's interlocutor is continuing to provide direction and interest. For beginners to performative writing, it has much to recommend it. Here I include but one exemplar, a dialogue with Kip Jones, whose stellar work we discussed in the opening chapter. Kip and I, along with several others, edited a special issue on performative social science in *FQS, Forum: Qualitative Social Research*, which is produced at the Free University in Berlin. I choose it for inclusion, especially, because its focus is on performative social science itself. We include as our alter ego a third character, the Cyber-Moderator, to direct and provoke the conversation.

REFLECTING ON PERFORMATIVE SOCIAL SCIENCE

Cyber-Moderator:	Social scientists are beginning to explore their own creativity. We encourage this, but should we also acknowledge the limitations of an individual to produce outputs that are professional enough to reach audiences and withstand scrutiny? Are skills and craft necessary components of this new method? How is all of this "evaluated"?
Mary:	When I hear the word "creativity," I imagine the aesthetic world: artists at their easels, sculptors chiseling away at blocks of marble, actors proclaiming lines of Shakespeare,

and musicians, poets, and novelists creating new artistic pieces, often alone in their studios. But then I remind myself that scientists have a lore of creativity as well, which stretches far back in time. Each strand of creativity is revered within its own discipline, but the two streams seem quite separate from one another. The visual artist, musician, or writer live in the world of fantasy and fiction (with internal norms according to the "group" with which they are identified), while the scientist's creativity is identified within the strict confines of an established discipline, which is bound by rules, laws, and strict protocols of behavior. I think the crossover that we have witnessed in this special issue of *FQS* has heralded the bridging of the two streams of creativity. Both the aesthetic means as promoted by those we call artists, and social science concerns as advanced by scientists, are melded into a unified whole.

Yes, they are there, but, as you ask, is the artistic side of the equation good enough to be appreciated by today's audiences? One might equally pose the question as to whether a good performance piece, with fascinating aesthetic quality, is sufficient as a work of science, as judged by contemporary standards of the scientists. Clearly to become a highly appreciated artist, one usually must work very hard at the craft and use all forms of connivance and collusion to make a dent in the highly competitive world of art, as I have heard about it secondhand. And an equally arduous path awaits the ambitious scientist, eager to find a journal in which to publish a manuscript. What is the balance that is needed, as a social scientist, to be accepted in the sciences, while producing an aesthetic piece? Given the competitive nature of both strands and the expectations of the audience, it might seem that the project of Performative Social Science (PSS) is doomed to failure. Yet this is not the case, and I think one reason for this is that the positioning of artistic modes of creativity together with issues and ideas familiar within the scholarly fields is in itself sufficiently novel and illuminating that no one seems to mind if all the highest glory of either one is not attained in the crossover.

I think of a project in which people were interviewed about significant events in their lives: from the interview transcripts, researchers created poetic phrases taking the liberty of creating the emphasis that they thought the interviewees had projected in the tone of their voice, the redundancy of their comments, and their emotional expressiveness. Through altering the interview comments and using repetition, a deeper and more informative outcome was attained, one that was more useful in gaining understanding than a strict report of the interview statements would have been.

Ken Gergen and I have talked about the professionalism that is lacking in most artistic productions by social scientists. He takes the point of view that "amateurism" is more likely to spawn new productions and projects than a totally slick performance will. If the performers are too good, they suggest that only a special and gifted few are able to advance the PSS agenda. I tend to agree, but there have been some performances, especially when we did a five-year-long annual symposium at the American Psychological Association called Performative Psychology, when I thought the line had been crossed between amateurish and embarrassing. How amateurish can we be and still be taken seriously? That's the question that is taunting us all, I would say.

Kip: You bring up many points that I have also been considering. "Amateur and embarrassing productions" is one that I have often worried over. I have referred before to these kinds of productions as the Mickey and Judy response: "I know what we'll do! We'll put on a show!" I doubt that in those movies Rooney or Garland ever actually raised enough cash to save the farm. It is also worrying that social scientists' knee-jerk response to the "performative" is too often to put on a play. There is a plethora of tools from the arts that can be explored to fit the research itself and the potential audience. I would suggest considering other media, particularly new media. Could your paper become a radio play, for example? Or could it be turned into an open-scripted community event with participants moving from audience to performer and back again? In the end, could the audience "write" the play? How could the paper be represented visually? Could it be danced without words? Is there music that comes to mind when you think about the narrative, and how could this be used to montage the story aurally?

Mary: In terms of evaluation, all evaluation is from some standpoint, and some forms have longer, clearer, and more accepted histories than others. You fail or pass A levels in the UK, and in the United States we have a combined score for your SAT's of 1600 or less. When it comes to artistic ability or social skills, we are on shakier grounds. I don't think anyone doing performative social science would claim that there are conventional standards by which to judge a piece. It is an open question. Perhaps we don't want to come to a conclusion about what counts as good or bad. Perhaps we would like to leave it open, in the realm of the relational—that is, the reactions of people who engage with the performative piece is what counts. And then, that too is open to response. In general, I think we don't want the performance creators to have the last word, nor the actors or audience, nor the reviewers or critics. That said, journal editors, colleagues, hiring and tenure committees, and other gatekeepers will have their says. That is the way of the world. Should there be a last word? Whose should it be?

Kip: Standards for "judging" performative work need to be found within contemporary aesthetics. We would not scrutinize textual production of social science by standards from fifty or one hundred years ago, so why would we do that with aesthetics? In postmodern times, should we be "judging" or evaluating at all? Wouldn't it be better to think in terms of how a production is communicating with local communities, contributing to conviviality, even change? Is the audience's experience enough? How are they relating and responding to us? When we move to the performative as researchers, we cede "control" over the interpretation of our work to our audience. This is the singularly most important shift in social science practice that PSS makes. Ironically and at the same time, we gift ourselves with the opportunity to be more interpretive, more intuitive, more creative, in our outputs. Our job is not so much to convince as to provoke and stimulate.

           The reality is that social scientists may very well feel that their skills are inadequate to move into the realm of the arts and media production. This is where collaboration becomes central to this new movement. By forming partnerships with practitioners from the arts, we again "cede control" of our work and open up the possibility of further interpretation by others.

Having explored this in workshop circumstances, I see a clear division in ways of proceeding. The social scientist tends to want to spend a lot of time thinking and talking about what s/he might do to expressively interpret her/his work; the artist tends to grab tools and materials and begin to experiment and play with concepts and possibilities. Learning to work in this creative way is a lesson worth learning if social scientists want to work creatively and productively. Perhaps a "guilty pleasures" example: the TV fashion design programs, Project Runway (US version) or Project Catwalk (UK version), give budding designers a challenge project in each episode. The artists make sketches of their ideas first, usually for about ten minutes. The rest of the allotted time (about two days) is spent *creating* their vision. The process of *doing* is the creative endeavor. This lesson is crucial for social scientists wishing to engage in creative undertakings of their own making.

It is not impossible for social scientists to expand their skill and craft in creative ways of developing their work. This takes some humility and the ability to embrace "not knowing." If we want to produce visually, learn to see better; if we want to work with sound, learn to hear better; if we want to use physicality, get to know our bodies better. Most of all, these efforts will allow us to look beyond the narrow confines of our own disciplines to the wider world, even worlds other than our own. I know that I personally have learned more about producing performative social science, for example, by watching Kylie Minogue than by reading Judith Butler. If "camp" can be seen as a production technique, then I certainly owe more to the former than the latter. I remain steadfastly committed to a fusion between popular culture and serious scholarship in order to reach wider audiences with my own work.

Thinking performatively is about putting aside that analytical part of ourselves that normally deals with data and such, and moving to the other side of the equation and getting in touch with that earlier place where we were energized by the data itself—how it was sparking ideas that were coming from our own personal experience, which, as every creative person will tell you, is the fount of all creativity. It's also about communication; it's about how we are going to develop our skills in collaborating with someone who is speaking a different language, coming from a different background. Going through that learning process is almost as important as the end product itself. Where I see people going a bit off is when they want to sit and talk about "what is Truth" and other cerebral gymnastics that we all do all the time anyway. In reality, it's more about how do we find our creative impulse and how can we contribute that to the experience. It isn't the end production, really. Ultimately, is it possible to collaborate and produce something creatively that is better than having research printed in a journal? It's one of those either/or things and you may walk away and say, "I'd rather have my material printed in a journal," and that's one answer. If, however, you're interested in tapping into a zeitgeist in a wider arena than just standard scholarship, PSS is one way to go.

Cyber-Moderator: Both artists and researchers typically work in isolation. How do we encourage cooperation, collaboration, and dialogue across disciplines? How do we facilitate creative encounters and relationships between artists and researchers that will lead to joint efforts and outputs? Is a community (physical or virtual) necessary in order to produce this work?

Mary: Indeed, I think that there must be those who engage in brokering arrangements that cross disciplines. Conferences, online exemplars, small group gatherings in academic settings across disciplinary boundaries, all are needed. Journals such as *Qualitative Inquiry* and, of course, *FQS* in particular, are helpful in providing models of what might be possible for the weak of heart. The activities that you, Kip, and your online and live colleagues have been promoting are central to this mission.

Today, looking at the Performsocsci@jiscmail.ac.uk listserv I was delighted to see that new interdisciplinary degrees are being created that merge the interests of people who are eager to participate across some boundaries that separate the performative and the scientific. For example, an MA in Media Ethnography is being considered at the Art and Design Research Institute at Manchester Metropolitan University. What does the future portend for the students taking such a degree? Will they find work or a nonacademic activity that will be advanced by this type of education? Is this type of program a foolhardy endeavor or a harbinger of the next wave in our culture?

Kip: Interesting that you bring up that particular offering at MMU, Mary. The organizer, Amanda Ravitz, a visual anthropologist, was one of the facilitators in Bournemouth's workshop series in PSS. Interesting because this demonstrates how PSS is moving forward and becoming more solidly embedded in academic practice. Another example: I am now working with postgrad students from the Media School here at Bournemouth and I have been offered a cross-school appointment in order to bring the two worlds together, Health and Social Science and Media. "Ambiguity" seems to be moving into the Academy then!

Cyber-Moderator: Kip mentions the word "ambiguity." He seems to like this as a word and concept, but what does it mean? By building ambiguity into our productions, are we further fueling audience participation in discovery of meaning? Or are we simply blurring the boundaries of our outputs because we are unsure of their meaning?

Mary: I suspect a bit of tongue in cheek here as you ponder the lack of clarity in the meaning of the term ambiguity. What if building in ambiguity was an attempt both to help the audience to discover new meanings and to signal our own lack of certainty? Or what if it was sometimes one and sometimes the other?

Kip: Well, "ambiguity" actually came up recently at a funder's consultation event in terms of "predicting" what the outputs might be for future research, and this is, of course, always an exercise in the ambiguous. The delight was in the fact that we were actually admitting to it! Since it was a roomful of mostly creative types, the audience seized upon the word and decided to work with it, rather than against it. We agreed that researchers/artists could gain a great deal from the concept of ambiguity as a method. "Findings" in the traditional sense would be sidelined or even banished. Dissemination would become method. Researchers would move from the safety of "knowing" to the uncertainty of "not knowing." Data would return to its place of importance as a resource for explorations of multiple understandings and a key for further engagement by wider communities beyond the Academia. Knowledge would be constructed socially in a relational way within a participatory society. The researcher would become a gatherer, a facilitator, a curator, a Wizard of Oz. Text would become only one tool within a toolbox of many instruments. Silence would be golden.

Mary: A different "take" on this concept is to suggest that ambiguity never is the product of one "author," but is always already in relation to others who are involved in the performance. One might even try to leave the door open to an ambiguous reading, but find that it is shut without anyone even noticing that there were other options for interpretation. Isn't it also the case that sometimes an interpretation of something you created is far from what you thought you did, but then you can also see the path by which the other found that meaning? I have had that happen to me. Do you see a relational approach as one that might be a way of addressing this conundrum?

Kip: Yes, I agree with you on this from my own experience. I was writing recently about my Princess Margaret production in a piece entitled "How did I get to Princess Margaret? (And how did I get her to the World Wide Web?)":

> When I used to paint pictures (I would say "for a living," except that there is not much of a living to be made from painting pictures), the thing that always amazed me was how viewers would/could put themselves into the pictures' stories and relate to the paintings personally. These narrative canvasses usually chronicled something from my private life—and this created the irony of this phenomenon. (Jones 2007)

This is exactly what I mean when I talk about ceding control of interpretation to the audience. Academically speaking, we could then talk about Bourriaud's relational aesthetics and how relational art is located in human interactions and their social contexts. (I have written at length about this elsewhere: see Jones 2006.) When at its best, this is what PSS is doing or attempting to do.

Cyber-   Shakespeare wrote: "Talkers are no great doers."
Moderator: How does that apply in the sense of research dissemination that moves "beyond text"?

Mary: You are suggesting that one of the advantages of performative work is that it extends beyond "just talk" to something more akin to doing. In some sense, I think we never move beyond text, even in the midst of intense action, but that is only because action is defined as being meaningful . . . and thus rich in symbolic significance. However, performative work is more than talk, and it is potentially more interactive than listening or reading. So it does seem that it is ahead of the game in terms of being a doing, rather than just a talking.

Kip: Yes, and it is the artist's inclination to "do" that I referred to earlier. If we want to be creative in our outputs, we will need to engage in a paradigm shift from talking to doing: moving beyond text and words and employing the power of sound, movements, and pictures, all moving towards the development of the potential of alternative means of communication of social science data. This makes it possible to *return* to the text with a much more creative and playful concept of its potential. Think Kerouac, Burroughs, and others or, even earlier than that, Stein and Joyce.

Cyber-Moderator: Does PSS "fit" within a larger framework of research and natural "shifts" that are already occurring in academic study and research? Where are the "new PSS" researchers coming from? Why is this happening now?

Kip: What fascinates me is how shifts and changes occur simultaneously, often globally, within and across various disciplines. I am convinced that it is when one discipline is "talking" to another that these shifts begin. Sometimes, collaborating across disciplines also comes into play. One shift in higher education in recent years has been an engagement in postgraduate study by older, more seasoned students. This often means that these students bring with them life and work experience from outside the confines of the particular academic discipline of their current study. These postgrad students cannot necessarily be led down one linear academic path, and they are more willing to engage with thinking "across disciplines" and bring to their efforts experiences from outside the walls of Academia. Those particularly attracted to PSS in higher education include people with backgrounds and experience from the media, as painters, musicians, etc., who are now engaged under the wide umbrella of social science scholarship in some way. These are the initial pioneers of PSS who bring both the utility and creative problem-solving skills of their arts-based backgrounds to their academic pursuits. These are the same people who saw standard PowerPoint presentations and said, "Hey! We can do this better!"

Mary: I do agree with you, Kip. I hadn't thought about the influence of older students, who do bring with them a fuller array of experiences than the traditional younger student. I also think that the influence of postmodern thinking has been important. One of the ideas that I think is influencing the borderland borrowings is that there is skepticism about the necessity of a special form that presentations must take on. Rather, there is no sacred language that must be used in order to engage in disciplinary work. Being able to step back and question why an article must be written in a particular way or why the line must be drawn between poetry and prose, or why first person indicators must be avoided—all become open to question.

Cyber-Moderator: How have rapid changes in technology contributed to the evolution of PSS? Is PSS a reaction to technology or a beneficiary? We seem to bounce between worldwide anonymous audiences for our efforts and local audiences and communities, encounters very anchored in a restricted space, place, and time. Should we be working at both the macro and micro level, or is one more important than the other?

Kip: I am intrigued at the moment by working on both levels simultaneously. An example: sometimes people from Australia, Canada, or the United States will email me when we are putting on a master class or workshop in PSS here at Bournemouth in the U.K. and ask: "Can you put the event on the web so that we can watch from here?" My gut reaction is no, it is not the same thing. These are local events, and it is in the participation that the work is accomplished. These are not "lectures" in any traditional academic sense. The majority of the time is spent "doing," as discussed earlier. On the other hand, I had no problem at all in making a short film about the experience of the workshops, interviewing some participants and "teasing" the audience with visuals representing some of the activities—without being prescriptive. This was in order to encourage the audience to consider these possibilities for themselves, what *they* could do, think about what *their* workshops might be like, and so forth. The video has been viewed over one thousand times so far. This is but one example where micro/macro becomes clearer for me. (Parenthetically, this is also an example of an output produced through collaboration with a professional filmmaker.)

Mary: I think you raise the challenge of how to be micro when macro. You resist it, but also seem to be doing it. There is something about the face-to-face interactions that are generally so much more fulfilling on an embodied/personal level. Yet, I also think that you underestimate the creative potential in just seeing the short film you did about the experience. There are many ways that viewers might expand or be influenced by your film other than replicating a workshop format. Perhaps they will take one piece of it to their classroom, or explore new ways of relating to a friend, etc.

There is something positive about keeping a trace of a performance, even if it involves more passivity on the part of the viewer. In terms of my own performances, one of the regrets I had over the years (and I'm talking years since the early 1980s) was that after the "show" was over, it was over. There was nothing left to hold on to. Sometimes there were photographs or perhaps a short video, but still, this desire for some permanence was unfulfilled. (Of course, there was another part of me that wondered if I had too much desire for recognition or résumé-building going on, and that it was better for the world and my character to just let things come and go. Sometimes I was even glad that the performance had disappeared into thin air.)

I have another regret in doing single performances. I do feel that I am shutting down conversation and critique by performing. In another work I'd like to figure out a way to include the audience as actors. I'm not sure that solves the problem. The totality of the form does not welcome intrusion. It would be messy. I'm not sure if I am "onto something" here or not.

Kip: I definitely think that you have hit upon a crucial element in the future development of PSS: allowing for intrusions, shocks, and surprise endings by focusing the development and production of performative pieces on the audience as the final interpreter, interlocker, magician, sage. This is where the politics becomes profoundly embodied;

the evocative transforms into the provocative; and the possibility of social science research's contributing to changing hearts and minds becomes a reality.

Cyber-Moderator: Is a redefinition of the "public space" of research necessary in order to benefit from this movement? Has the community of recipients of research widened because of this new public space?

Mary: I feel that some form of democratization has been going on in all areas of life since the 1960s. There have been ups and downs, of course, but the trend is there, and although it sounds good when I call it democratization, it is less than good when one considers some of the consequences: any kid can get a gun and go to school with it (an American example); it isn't difficult in some housing projects in the Middle East to be trained to blow oneself up and destroy the order of some mighty military command; it isn't hard to put a movie of yourself on YouTube, or write your opinion on a blog. Don't you think that this opening of the public space for all people in all venues has varied consequences for performative research?

Kip: The agora has always existed and "public space" has always been used performatively for various purposes. I don't think that making use of public space is as much needed as it is a need for academics to reach wider audiences; part of this has to do with research funders who are no longer so interested in "outputs" as they are in "outcomes." Outcomes mean, what meaningful effects do our research projects have on the wider world, or at least on the very segment of the population that we are "studying"? Secondly, these same funders want this information to reach a wider audience, not just a narrow academic and/or policy audience. This creates a scramble around widening means of dissemination of research findings that is quite new.

The democratization of the Internet was built into the medium from the outset. This means that the medium will include the good, the bad, and the ugly. Democracy also means choice. There are no ticket takers or gate-keepers on the Internet, try as some may. The Internet is the global water cooler. As far as dissemination is concerned, my own experiments with uploading my videos to the net have proved quite interesting. Thousands have now viewed them. The same material in published format would never have reached such a large and varied audience. In fact, I have little idea of who my audience is. This is part and parcel of, again, ceding "control" over my outputs and putting my trust in the audience. I do know that some of the videos are being used for classes, Blackboard, etc. Otherwise, like Norma Desmond, I just put my faith in "those wonderful people out there in the dark."

8

Juxtaposing Genres

Ken Gergen

Explorations into multiple voicings are significant, not simply because they enrich and expand the potentials of what can be communicated in a piece of writing, but also because they deconstruct the concept of the author as a solitary and originary source of what is written. They demonstrate that writing occurs within continuing traditions of relationship. Much more will be said about relational process—one of our chief scholarly interests—as the book progresses. However, to expand the possibilities of multiplicity, I tried in the following piece to work with multiple genres, or forms of writing. By using them in brief segments, there would be no overarching "voice of truth." By juxtaposing these segments, each genre would give way to the next, and its meaning thus be altered. Further, the hope was that the different genres could carry different rhetorical weight, thus enhancing the total impact of the writing.

The following is a short excerpt from my book *Relational Being: Beyond Self and Community* (2009b), a work that includes academic writing alongside autobiography, everyday talk, poetry, quotations from others, photographs, cartoons, and more. The following piece is less rich, but hopefully will illustrate the potential of juxtaposing genres. The content of the writing is part of a larger argument against dualism—the very idea of minds residing in bodies—and a preparation for reconstructing mental life as a relational activity. The reader may also find it interesting to compare this experiment in writing with similar ideas realized in the dramatic performances of the next section.

THE VERY IDEA OF SELF-KNOWLEDGE

In children's magazines we often find puzzles of the following sort: A number of words appear in one column, and in an adjoining column we find an equal number of pictured objects. The child is asked to match the word with the proper object, "tree" with a picture of a tree, "eagle" with a picture of an eagle, and so on. Each word refers to a particular kind of object. Now, as an adult, consider this possibility: Place a dozen words for mental states in a column, words like "love," "hope," "attitude," and "intention." In an adjoining column sketch a picture of these various states. When you have assembled the puzzle . . . "Hold on . . ." you say, "you want 'pictures' of mental states. What do you mean?" Yes, what could I possibly mean?

What is the color of love, the shape of hope, the size of an attitude, the contour of an intention? The questions seem nonsensical; they leave us speechless. But why are they nonsensical? For one, because whatever we mean by "an inner world," it is not like the "outer world." There is nothing in the "inner world" that allows us to make a picture of it, nothing equivalent to saying, "That is an apple, and it is red." If you close your eyes, and focus all your attention within, what precisely are you looking at? And if your eyes are closed, what are you using to do the looking?

•

In his *Discourse on Method*, René Descartes set out to locate a foundational reality, a solid ground from which he could proceed to understand the nature of life. Descartes found good reason to doubt the opinion of authorities, the claims of his peers, and even the evidence conveyed to him by his senses. Yet, he could not doubt the existence of his own doubting . . . the fact that he was thinking. Yet, we must ask, how did Descartes know that he was *thinking*? What precisely is "a thought," that he could be sure he had one? What is the color, the shape, the size, the diameter, or the weight of a thought? What if Descartes was simply speaking silently to himself? Could he have mistaken his use of public speech for private thought? Could Descartes know he was doubting before he had acquired the public discourse of doubt?

•

Few ideas are both as weighty and as slippery as the notion of the self.
—Jerrold Seigel

•

Sigmund Freud proposed that the most significant content of the mind—our fundamental desires, deepest fears, and most unsettling memories—

are hidden from consciousness. This was a momentous proposal, not only launching the profession of psychiatry, but also laying the groundwork for much therapeutic practice since that time. Most important, Freud informed Western culture that we cannot know our own minds. What we want most to know is hidden beneath layers of repression.

Beneath a rational thought lies an unconscious desire.
Beneath professed love we may find hatred.
Beneath a wish to improve the world may lie the desire to destroy it.

Could Freud be right? On what grounds can he be refuted? And yet, how did Freud know these things? How could he peer into himself and recognize what lies beyond consciousness? How did he go about distinguishing between a repression, a desire, or a wish? What are the characteristics of these states that he could single them out? And, curiously, how did Freud manage to remove the barrier of repression to reveal the true nature of his own desires?

•

> *A great many people think they are thinking when they are merely*
> *rearranging their prejudices.*
> —William James

•

Let me propose that when you . . .
share your *thoughts* with me,
tell me you *love* me,
reveal to me your *hopes*,
tell me what *excites* you,
share your *fears* of the future,
declare that this is your *opinion*,
tell me that you *understand*,
report on what you *remember*,

you are *not* reporting on the state of a private world. Our words do not appear to name anything about which we can be certain. As we shall see, this is not their function.

•

I have pondered these matters for many years, and not without problems. Early in my marriage, Mary asked that we exchange words of devotion before winding into sleep at night. To hear "I love you" would be the reassurance necessary for tranquility. Such a simple request . . . and yet I was tormented. How could I be certain of my mental state . . . how could I peer inward to know precisely the nature of my emotions . . . did emotions exist in the mind or in the body or somewhere else? I labored nightly for an answer that would allow a clear declaration. Finally, one night, exhausted by my interminable philosophizing, Mary intoned, "Just say the words . . .!" This I was all too happy to do, and we have slept soundly ever since.

9

Reflections on Writing

Ken: We have been playing at the edge of possibilities for social science writing for some time now, and I wonder what we might have learned from our efforts. Where have they succeeded or failed, in our eyes; what might we do differently; where are the joys and the discomforts? For example, one of the things I have felt particularly pleased about are those cases in which the form of writing instantiates or expresses its content. We are so accustomed to approaching a piece of writing in terms of its content or message, without realizing that the form of the writing also conveys a message. Sometimes the message embedded in the form can even negate the content. In any case, it is exciting to explore ways of synchronizing content and form in such a way that the former is enriched and strengthened. I am not sure how successful we were in our attempts, but for me the Duography piece was a real breakthrough. That we could challenge the individualism embodied in the concept of the autobiography by launching a duography gave me a lot of pleasure. By the end, when we tried to find a way of blurring the identity of the authors behind the voices—suggesting that there are no truly independent persons—I was in heaven.

Mary: I guess if you were in heaven, so was I . . . especially if we are considering the blurring of identities as an outcome of the voicing. I also feel that playing with the texts, using various forms, changing fonts, sizes, page lengths, margins, and including photographs, drawings, and other visual things, changes the nature of the writer's relationship with the reader. These changes suggest you are performing for the reader, anxious to reach him or her. Recently I have been an external examiner for a couple of PhD dissertations, and in each case performance was an integral part of the project. Recall, for example, the "box" dissertation created by Zoë Fitzgerald-Pool, described in chapter 2. I have also read a dissertation that depended heavily on the examiner's listening to a CD of music, which illustrated the means by which the researcher had interacted with her participants. Both dissertations came from social science programs, not from the humanities or fine arts. And both reached out to me, intrigued me, and invited me into new spaces of appreciation.

Ken: This really speaks to the problem with traditional writing that we described in the early chapters. Where traditional writing generally places a wedge between author and audience, performative writing seems to be more like a "gift" for the reader. At the same time, I don't think that performative writing necessarily draws author and reader closer. It is clearly the case that some of the writing we have just shared has an academic audience in mind. And even the academic traditionalists might be put off by the wordplay, often at their expense. So, there is no guarantee that in doing performative work you will automatically reach an audience.[1]

Mary: This is also interesting because we often have multiple audiences in mind, and differing hopes for them. I think there are times we want to criticize the more rigid defenders of the faith, that is traditional writers, and at the same time woo those with whom we feel aligned. The various dissertations I've read that go in the performative direction seemed to me to be trying to reach out to their readers, but what are the readers hoping for? In the case of the dissertation with the recorded music attached, the singing was designed to convey the emotional tone present in the music workshop in which the songs were created. I, for one, felt both drawn to the work and illuminated by the music, but could imagine others who would find it needlessly stuck onto the writing. One can imagine how much more powerful it would be to hear someone speaking about their experiences than reading a copy of the transcript, especially if scripted by conversation analysts, in which strange symbols must be learned to get a sense of the pauses, repetitions, guttural sounds, etc. that people use when talking. One could even suggest that conversation analysis could be "saved" by a turn to the performative.

Ken: At the same time, I sometimes worry about the patience of social science readers to work through a writerly text. We are trained to search for content, and the more rapidly we find it, the more rapidly we can move on to a production phase. We have learned to read instrumentally. So, a real question for the future of performative work is whether the academic audience will stop to truly engage. I have witnessed a similar resistance in the case of much narrative research, and autoethnography. Readers are interested enough to see that a given piece has been published, but they are less willing to take the time to read it. Since the work is not cumulative in the traditional sense, but rather "expressive," as one might say, it is not essential that one grasp its content.

Mary: And this raises the whole question of whether performance work has much in the way of cumulative potentials. Does it exhaust its implications in the "performative moment?" But perhaps the whole idea of accumulation in the social sciences—a kind of monetary metaphor in any case—is problematic. Ah, the beginning of another discussion . . .

Figure 1

Figure 2

Figure 3

Figure 4

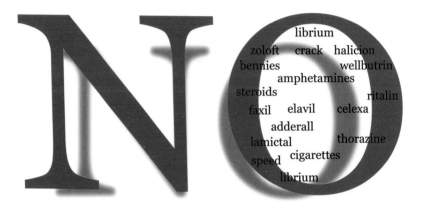

Figure 5

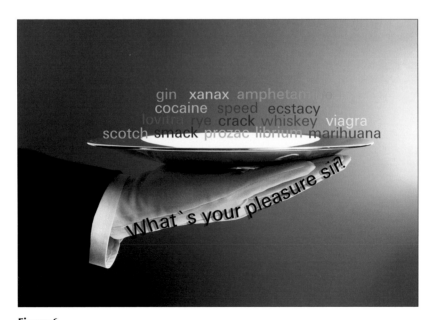

Figure 6

SECTION III

DRAMATIC ARTS: IDEAS IN ACTION

S peaking is essentially a social performance. As we speak we address others, with the expectation that their actions will be coordinated with ours. If we went about speaking to no one, we might be judged mad; if others' actions were not coordinated with ours, we would fail to "make sense." But the words are only partial performances. The quality of the voice—its volume, rapidity, and tone—is essential to the performance, along with facial features, gestures, and posture. Compared to the richly laden practice of everyday communication, most social science writing is indeed impoverished. The text is addressed to no one in particular and without any obvious context; the coordinated actions from which the life of the text is generated are not in view; and the words themselves circulate without an attached body. For the scholarly community, writing can have especially deadening effects. We appear to each other not as fully embodied creatures, but as ghostly mentalities. We write into a social vacuum, bereft of the corporal coordination that brings life to language. There is ample reason, then, to move beyond dry and deadly forms in our scholarly work, and to return language to its vital place in the embodied dramas of relationship. It is against this background that the two of us have set out to explore ways of realizing scholarly ideas in theatrical performances. The drama of attempting to do drama is perhaps a chapter in itself. In what follows, however, we share a number of attempts that have given pleasure to us, and we hope to our various audiences. Alas, with the limitations of print media, we can only share the verbal skeletons. We can only invite the readers to let their imagination roam freely.

10

Performing the Mind

Ken Gergen

As outlined in chapter 2, for us there is a close association between a social constructionist view of knowledge and the performative turn. From a constructionist standpoint, what we count as the real and the good is generated within relationships or communities of practice. This would include what we take to be the reality of mind. If it is only by convention that we presume the existence of minds—of thought, motivation, emotion, and the like—then "mind talk" is fundamentally optional. That is, we are free to generate alternative accounts of the person. Why should one take up such a challenge? According to the traditional view, our minds are private possessions—inside our heads—and the primary source of our actions. However comfortable this Western view may be, it is also a tradition that divides us. It suggests that I am living inside my mind, you within yours. We are fundamentally isolated and alienated. I am the master of my own actions; you should not interfere. I am seeking the ends that I desire, and you likewise. If we collaborate, it is only because it allows us to better fulfill our private desires. Fundamentally it is a war of all against all, but if we can make necessary agreements, and if we have moral injunctions to help our neighbors, then cultural life may be viable. In effect we create a culture pervaded by loneliness, manipulation, exploitation, anxiety, and ruthlessness.

How else could we understand human action, and its source? What if we could understand ourselves as fundamentally relational beings, never alone or isolated, and treat the processes of thinking, feeling, wanting, and so on as constituents of a relational process? What if my ability to speak of my choices, intentions, loves, beliefs, hopes, and so on was a gift of my participating in a cultural history? Would this not mean a dramatic transformation in our daily life, and in our institutions? A full account of this adventure into reconstruction is contained in my book, *Relational Being: Beyond Self and Community* (K. J. Gergen 2009b).

For now, I wish to share some of the performative work that has resulted from this approach. First, consider the following: when we speak or write about our minds, we typically use language referentially. That is, we talk about our intentions, beliefs, ideas, emotions, needs, and so on as if the terms referred to events or states inside the head. The same is true of psychological science. One studies cognition, emotion, motivation, and the like as if these were actual states or activities, and research can somehow provide an accurate map or picture of the internal world. However, if language is essentially social performance, attention shifts away from the referents of such terms to the way the language of the mind functions within relational action. In effect, we may view psychological discourse as action performed within a relationship. The challenge for me has been to illuminate these ideas dramatically.

For the most part, these experiments in drama have taken place in colloquia, classrooms, workshops, and at conferences—all contexts of face-to-face relations. While the major share of the presentation is "straight academic talk," the performative work is inserted into the presentation in much the same way as one might a PowerPoint presentation. However, in this case the dramatic performances are intended to bring the ideas to life: essentially, to embody theory. The dramatizations are used in two major ways, first to undermine the longstanding presumption that psychological language refers to activities in a mental world, and second, to demonstrate the way mental discourse functions in human relationships. In other words, the episodes function both deconstructively and reconstructively. At the same time, the dramatizations try to realize some of the potentials of a performative social science. In the two following sections I include examples of both deconstructive and reconstructive performances, along with a bit of conceptual context.

DILEMMAS OF DUALISM

Does our mental language actually refer to specific states of mind? What kinds of problems do we generate if we presume that there are minds inside our heads? Consider some classical and contemporary problems raised by philosophers, problems that remain largely unsolved today. One of the peskiest problems is how the mind ever acquires knowledge of the world outside, how the "outside" ever makes its way to the "inside." The philosopher John Locke proposed that knowledge is built up through observation. We enter the world with our minds approximating "blank slates"; we know nothing. We begin to fill the slate through observation. Locke's view forms the basis of empiricist science today. But consider a mother teaching her "blank slate" son about the world:

Mother: Look Tommy, look at the bird.
Tommy: . . . [stares aimlessly about]
Mother: Tommy, look quickly, the bird is hopping away.
Tommy: . . . [continues his aimless stare]
Mother: Oh Tommy, but now see, they are selling balloons. Wouldn't you like a red balloon?
Tommy: . . . [begins to wander off looking at nothing in particular]

In effect, if we enter the world with a blank slate mentality, what could possibly draw our interest in one direction as opposed to another? How would we ever acquire such mental categories as "bird" or "balloon"? It's all a booming buzzing confusion without any means or motivation to order. In fact, in the above case, Tommy wouldn't have a clue that there is a mother who is talking with him. It's all part of a moving flux.

Philosophers and psychologists have long labored with this problem, and perhaps their major solution is to propose that we must have some rudimentary concepts or categories upon birth. We build on these through experience. Thus, Immanuel Kant proposed a number of *a priori* categories, such as causality and number. Noam Chomsky (1968) argued for an inherent storehouse of rudimentary linguistic knowledge. So, let's see what happens when we grant such knowledge to the child. Let's play God and grant to Tommy some rudimentary mental categories such as "feels good/feels bad," "up/down," and "in/out." We return to his mother's attempt to hasten Tommy's mental development:

Mother: Tommy, Tommy . . .
Tommy: Feels good.
Mother: Oh Tommy, dear [smiling], that's your name.
Tommy: Up.
Mother: Oh, silly boy, up is a direction [pointing upward].
Tommy: In.
Mother: [now a little irritated] Tommy . . . "in" is a place, like "in the box". . . Now pay attention!
Tommy: Up.
Mother: No, Tommy, no . . . [shaking her finger]
Tommy: In.
Mother: [in exasperation] . . . Oh Tommy, you are just being naughty; now try to pay attention.

Tommy: Feels bad.
Mother: [smilingly] Oh, I think you've got it. Yes, it does feel bad when you are just making me unhappy. So, here's a kiss . . . [she embraces him and kisses his cheek]
Tommy: Feels bad.
Mother: No, this feels bad. [as she pushes him away brusquely]
Tommy: Up.
Mother: I give up . . . !

As you can see, simply having some a priori categories of mind doesn't solve the problem of acquiring knowledge. The categories would simply continue aimlessly on, disconnected from the world outside. One would have to know a good deal more about the world and its rules and demands in order to use such categories. Why, then, do we presume that because we have two forms of discourse—about the mind on the one hand, and the world on the other—we have two different worlds? As philosopher Richard Rorty (1981) proposed, when we presume these two realities we create a range of fundamentally insoluble problems.

Let's continue to explore these problems. Consider the difficulties we have in trying to understand how mental states can affect physical states. If I *decide* I want to cross the street, how is my mental decision converted into physical action? This was Descartes' problem as well, but no one has been able to make sense of his claim that the conversion takes place in the pineal gland. Now consider the following interchange at a doctor's office:

Client: Doc, I've got a problem.
Doctor: Please tell me about it . . .
Client: I wake up, and think of all the things I really have to do, and know I should get up, but then I just lie there . . .
Doctor: Don't you *want* to get up?
Client: Absolutely! I really want to. I think of all the things I need to accomplish, and all the terrible stuff that will happen if I don't get up. But I don't.
Doctor: But don't you feel guilty . . . just lying there like that?
Client: Sure I do. I just have to get up and I really feel terrible about it. But I just keep lying there, unable to move.
Doctor: Why not try to think of something that could reward you for your rising . . . something fun, or exciting?
Client: Yeah, that's a great idea, and as a matter of fact I try it all the time. I have the most wonderful fantasies about all sorts of great things. But still, I don't move a limb . . . So what's wrong, Doc?

Doctor: Well, in my opinion, you failed to solve the mind–body problem. You have a Cartesian catarrh.

Of course, in much of our daily talk we treat the mind–body problem as solved. We see no problem in talking about how beliefs, desires, fears, motives, intentions, and so on cause us to behave in the way we do. But it is just here that the philosopher Gilbert Ryle (1984) has raised a related problem. Consider the following discussion between two scientists in a cognitive science laboratory:

Ralph: I have to tell you about a fascinating finding, Frank. I just learned that a subject in my last study solved all the most difficult problems we presented to him. No one has ever done that.
Frank: Hmm . . . You're right, Ralph. What do you make of that, how do you explain it?
Ralph: Well, I really think this subject must be relying on a rapid information processing system.
Frank: Well, OK . . . But why does he process information so rapidly?
Ralph: Good question. One of the most obvious reasons is that he relies on rapid memory scanning.
Frank: Good enough . . . But why this? Why does he scan memory so fast?
Ralph: I suppose it is because he has processed the available information in an orderly way for scanning.
Frank: Yeah . . . But that still leaves me puzzled. How come he orders information in such an orderly way?
Ralph: I think research would suggest it is because he orders information hierarchically?
Frank: Very nice . . . But it seems to me we still don't know why he orders information like that.
Ralph: Good question. Why don't we apply for a research grant to explore this problem?

In effect, when we trace our actions to events in the head, we are still left with the question of why these events take place as they do. The mental event seems to explain just so long as we aren't curious to ask about what preceded or caused it. And if we continue to be curious we step into a corridor of infinite regress.

But what are mental states in any case? We have thousands of words for mental states and conditions. We speak endlessly of our feelings, thoughts, desires, aims, values, beliefs, intentions, and so on. But what is the origin of these terms? Are they required by the fact that there is *something there inside* that demands a name? And where is "there" in this case? Inside the head, the heart, the neurons, the hormones? How can we "look inward" and identify psychological states? We move now to a therapist's office.

Therapist: So what brings you in? What's on your mind?

Client: Doc, I got problems . . . married seventeen years, three children, but I got this problem about other women. I just keep chasin'em, sleepin with'em, my eyes always open to the next skirt . . . I need to stop this . . .

Therapist: Ok, but one thing that's very important . . . How do you feel about your wife? Do you love her?

Client: Well, I always *say* I do . . .

Therapist: That's not the point. Do you *really* love her . . .

Client: Well, I'm not so sure how to answer that . . . What exactly that means? . . . Are you asking if I do feel the same way I did back when we were courting?

Therapist: Not really. I am talking about now. Look deeply into yourself, your innermost feelings . . . Do you find love for her there?

Client: I don't know exactly what you mean. I mean, in terms of my body—all those deep yearnings—I do like sex with her, I really enjoy that . . .

Therapist: No, I am not just talking about sex! Let me put it another way. Do you really care about your wife's welfare, her happiness?

Client: Well, sure, I guess I do . . . But is that love? I mean, I also care about what happens to my buddies, people who are bad off . . . like starving . . . and even my dog. I think I am a pretty caring person . . .

Therapist: [a little irritated] Well, then let's just talk a little more about what kinds of things you do feel for your wife . . . Expand on that for me . . .

Client: Hmm . . . It's kind of hard to say . . . I don't really know . . . What if I said something like "angry"?

Therapist: Oh? Why anger?

Client: Well, it stands to reason, doesn't it? Look at all these things I do to her by being unfaithful. I must be boiling angry and wanting to get back at her.

Therapist: Interesting. But how do you know it's anger? Maybe you really love her, and your love is frustrated in some way . . . So then it turns into anger.

Client: Well, it could be, but also maybe I just worship her because she's so good, and I feel so bad about myself that sleeping around is just a way of proving I am bad.

Therapist: I wonder if you don't really feel insecure . . . Maybe your job, or your sense that your wife is somehow superior. And you may be like a lot of men who, in a sense, married their mother, and thus find her an improper sex object. But for me, the real question is whether you have enough love for your wife to get through this.

Client: . . . [silence]

As we find, "looking inward" doesn't yield any definitive answers. Or, to put it another way, the vast vocabulary of psychological states that we have constructed does not have its origins in our examining our minds. We don't have the words because we recognized states or conditions of mind that simply demanded these names.

We could also see from this last vignette that the therapist had difficulty in knowing what was on the client's mind. He could ask questions, but in the end could only rely on the clues that seemed to be buried in the client's utterances. This raises a more general question: what do we ever know about what's on another person's mind? For philosophers this is the perennial and unsolved problem of other minds: how can we know they exist, and if they exist, how can we know their states or conditions? Or, more simply, how can I ever understand what's "on your mind"? How can I know, for example, that the words you use to describe "what's on your mind" are used in the same way as the words I use? Perhaps when you use the word "depression," it is the same word I use in referring to "nostalgia," "wistful longing," or "reverie." There is ultimately no way we can compare because we can never witness the mental state to which the other's words refer. Let's see how this would work out in practice. We return to the therapist's office, and a new client begins to describe his problem:

Client: I am so upset. I feel so fluzzy, it just really gets me down. I don't know what to do.

Therapist: I am sorry, Mr. Brown, I just don't know what it means when you say "fluzzy." Tell me more. What's it like to feel fluzzy?

Client: You don't know? It's like whizzing around on some kind of magic carpet, or finding yourself suddenly swimming around in the belly of a giant whale.

Therapist: Very interesting . . . but I am still unclear about this fluzzy. Are you saying it's like depression, for example, I mean with all that helplessness you just described?

Client: Hmm . . . depression . . . I don't really know this term very well . . . It's so professional . . . I mean, is depression like being sad?

Therapist: Well, a little like sadness, but different . . . Let's say, like a sadness that you can't explain, and it just persists.

Client: I don't really know. Sometimes I feel a little blue, but it comes and goes. In fact, everything I feel just comes and goes. Even fluzziness.

Therapist: Ok, then let's try something less professional. Is fluzziness like anger?

Client: You mean like when I am trying to get to the bathroom and stub my toe? I sure am angry then.

Therapist: I would see this more as frustration.

Client: Hmm. Frustration is more like when I feel like sex and don't get any.

Therapist: You know, I don't think this is getting us anywhere. But let's pick up on what you said about when you feel angry. Tell me a little about when you feel fluzzy: when and where do you get these feelings?

Client: The last time I had it was on the bus on the way over here. Then, just after breakfast when I was reading the paper. And, oh yes, I was watching TV last night and had a bout.

Therapist: This is complicated. Let me ask in another way: what other feelings is fluzzy like? What is it similar to?

Client: [pausing] It's sort of like mamoola . . . but a little stronger, and you might say it is similar to rheezama, but a little lighter, not so green.

Therapist: Mamoola, rheezama! You are driving me crazy with these terms.

Client: Now maybe we are in the same boat. Do you know any good therapists?

In conclusion, the language of the mind can't be derived from what there is, and it cannot function to give others a picture of what's in our heads. But, once we agree on how to use the language, we can move merrily along. Now we turn to an alternative to the dualist view of minds within bodies.

PSYCHOLOGY AS RELATIONAL ACTION

Let us abandon the traditional view of mental discourse as a series of pictures of what goes on in the head or the heart. With Wittgenstein (1953), let us now look at language as action within a relationship. The meaning of a word depends on its use within "games" of language, and these games are lodged in turn within cultural traditions of living. According to this view, mental discourse acquires its meaning not from its relationship to the mental world it seems to represent, but from the way we use it in the rituals of daily life. To speak properly about our minds does not mean getting it right about what's going on inside, but to participate effectively within a cultural tradition. Consider, for example, the process of memory. What is it to remember? Don't bother "looking inside" to answer this question. Consider the social process. Little Dora returns from her first day of classes in her first year of school:

Mother: Dora, dear, I am so excited. Tell me what happened to you today.

Dora: I first put my right foot in front of the left, and then my left foot in front of my right, and my right foot in front of my left, and my . . .

Mother: [interrupting] No, dear, not your walking. What happened at school, what nice memories do you have?

Dora: I looked at the teacher's nose, and then I looked at her chin, and then I saw her teeth, and then I saw her dress, and . . .

Mother: [again interrupting, more spiritedly] Oh Dora, not what you looked at. Tell me about what happened, what you *did*?

Dora: Well, the teacher asked us if we knew the alphabet, and I raised my hand, and she called on me, and I knew it perfectly. I was so happy because not all the children knew the alphabet.

Mother: Oh, Dora, I am so proud of you. What a nice first day at school.

As we see, remembering properly is akin to having good manners; to remember correctly is to follow a social convention. Yet, to have a mind is not simply knowing when and how to talk. To express what's on one's mind is a fully embodied action. And, like language, to make sense one must participate in a cultural tradition. To illustrate, consider the following: Ernest's boss at work finds Ernest singularly unexpressive. A personal coach is hired to help Ernest become more fully communicative:

Coach: OK, Ernest, they tell me you aren't very expressive. Let's see about that. Join me in a role play. Imagine for a moment that your teenage son has taken the family car out without permission. He drinks a lot of beer with his friends, and on the way home smashes the car into a tree. Your son is fine, but the car is totally destroyed. So, show me how you respond to your son. What do you say to him?

Ernest: [in a faint, meek voice] I am really angry.

Coach: [disbelieving] No, you can't mean that! You really can't just say it like that. You have to say it with force, with volume. So, try again.

Ernest: [screaming in a high pitched voice] I AM REALLY ANGRY!

Coach: Well, yeah . . . impressive. But you can't scream like that. Sounds like you are castrated. Use a low voice, from way down in your lower jaw.

Ernest: [this time in a base voice, but grinning] I AM REALLY ANGRY!

Coach: Yeah, that's almost it. But what's that grin on your face. That just doesn't go. Clench your teeth, poke your jaw out. Try again.

Ernest: [following the coach's advice on facial expression] I AM REALLY ANGRY!

Coach: Well, that's much better. But you just can't *say* it, and it's not just your face that's important. You have to put your whole body into it. Try again.

Ernest: [lifting one foot into the air, and waving his hands over his head] I AM REALLY ANGRY!

Coach: No, no, no . . . That just looks weird. Try this: stand firm with your legs, lean your body slightly forward, clench your fists, and then try it.

Ernest: [following directions] I AM REALLY ANGRY!

Coach: Fantastic! You have it just right. You are a terrific learner.

Ernest: [repeating the preceding posture, voice, and facial expressions] I AM REALLY HAPPY!

So, we don't "have" emotions so much as we "do" them. Emotion is an action within a relationship. Like other actions with mental attributes, we can do them well or poorly, fully engaged or superficially. But why do them at all? It is not because there are neural or biological necessities. Rather, it is because they are ways of carrying out social traditions. We do them largely because they are sensible actions within ongoing relationships. If you see your child weeping, you are likely to be consoling. What else would you do, and still be intelligible? Consolation is an act within the social traditions in which we reside. Such actions also achieve something within our relationships. Now consider emotional terms and what they accomplish. We have, for example, dozens of words for states or conditions of attraction. This is not because we can somehow identify all these internal states or because brain scans differentiate among them. Rather, when enacted, they function socially in different ways. Consider the plight of a man who wants to know about the feelings of a woman he has taken out, and what follows from her various statements about her feelings:

Rashad: We've been going out for several weeks now, and I really don't know where we stand. I really need to know your feelings at this point . . .

Michelle: Frankly, Rashad, I feel a little *ambivalent* . . .

Rashad: That's disappointing. I guess I've been pushing too hard. I'll back off.

Rashad: We've been going out for several weeks now, and I really don't know where we stand. I really need to know your feelings at this point . . .

Michelle: I have to tell you Rashad, I feel *quite intrigued* by you . . .

Rashad: [laughing] Ah, the mysterious stranger. Hey, I feel the same about you . . . Let's go to the show at the art museum this weekend.

Rashad: We've been going out for several weeks now, and I really don't know where we stand. I really need to know your feelings at this point . . .

Michelle: Well Rashad, to tell you the truth, you really *get my juices going*, my motor purring.

Rashad: Yeah, mine too. Isn't this great? Why don't we get a room down in Atlantic City this weekend?

Rashad: We've been going out for several weeks now, and I really don't know where we stand. I really need to know your feelings at this point . . .

Michelle: To tell you the real truth, Rashad, I've never felt like this before . . . I am *totally in love* with you. I think you may be the love of my life.

Rashad: Yeah, I have to tell you that I was afraid of that. I just don't think I can take on that responsibility. I think we really need to cool it for a while.

None of Michelle's comments are accurate readings of her neurons; they are vital actions in a relationship. They invite the other to move in one way or another, closer or more distant as in Michelle's relationship to Rashad. Or to borrow from Wittgenstein, the range of our psychological vocabulary is the limit of what we can do together.

This also represents an argument against the popular idea that mental states are just another way of talking about brain functions. Or, as many therapists would have it, to cure behavior problems we must chemically treat the brain. The hope for many scientists is that we could ultimately explain all behavior in terms of the brain. But could we? What would become of social life if we used brain terminology in place of the popular idioms of psychology? Would courtship be the same without a discourse of love, or criminal justice be achieved without a discourse of voluntary decisions? Could such traditions be sustained if we simply substituted brain terms for our common vernacular? If, indeed, such a substitution were made, then the following conversation should be reasonable.

A married couple, Ruth and Jerry, are just finishing dinner together:

Ruth: There is something I just have to ask you, Jerry. We have been married now for three years, and I have begun to worry. Do you still love me?

Jerry: Oh, a good question Ruth, but not a good time to ask. I mean, we just finished eating and because I am busy digesting, my pulse is a bit elevated. But, hey, I just remembered. I have my annual physical check-up tomorrow, and I can ask Dr. Zilstein to give me an EKG. I will bring the EKG findings home tomorrow night. Maybe we can check it out.

Ruth: Oh, good, Jerry . . . That's very thoughtful. But [pausing], you know, an EKG is not very sensitive. I really think you should look into getting a brain scan. Can you ask your doctor about what it would take to get an MRI?

Jerry: Sure, Ruth . . . great idea . . . But that's not going to be covered by insurance, and it is going to cost us . . . At the same time, this is important. I think we will just have to dig into our savings on this one.

Ruth: It is absolutely important, Jerry. If we are going to have children this is essential. In fact, I really don't think you can stop at an MRI; they aren't perfect, you know. Ask about getting an EEG and a PET scan too.

Jerry: [a little meekly] Yes . . . yes . . . I guess I can ask about it . . . But how much is this going to cost? . . .

Ruth: And that's not all, Jerry! There is still another question: Do I love *you*? We absolutely have to know this too. Our whole future depends on it.

Jerry: [gulping] Well . . . er . . . I guess you are right. [pause] But we have to do it! Yes, even if it takes our whole savings. We have to face up to it. And Ruth [pausing again] . . . If it turns out that I love you, and we find that you love me too, do you think we could have sex again?

This is brain talk taken to its absurd extreme. Yet, when psychologists begin to explain common mental terms in professional language, they also begin to undermine the traditions of social life. But the traditions can also be resistant. Consider the following attempts by Peter to explain his feelings in professional terms:

Cynthia: How do you really feel about me, Peter?

Peter: Truthfully, Ruth, you really stimulate my selfish genes.

Cynthia: And all this time I thought you really cared. I am out of here . . .

Cynthia: How do you really feel about me, Peter?

Peter: To tell you the truth, I don't know . . . I just have a lot of unexplained arousal, but I guess because of the scent of your perfume I am labeling it romantic.

Cynthia: That's really lame. Next time I will wear insect repellent . . . if there is a next time.

Cynthia: How do you really feel about me, Peter?

Peter: These antidepressants really upped my serotonin levels, so frankly I don't know if I feel happy because I'm with you, or with my prescription.

Cynthia: Goodbye, Peter! Next time I hope you can go out with a druggist.

Beware brain talk: it can be injurious to your well-being.

COACTION AND SCENARIOS OF PSYCHOLOGICAL LIFE

There yet remains a central ingredient to add to this emerging account of relational action. We must specifically consider the way in which meaning originates not from within isolated minds, but within a relational process. If I offer a greeting as you pass me in the street, it doesn't count as a greeting until you respond in a way that defines it in this way. If you respond with, "Hi, nice to see you," you have acknowledged that my utterance was a greeting. If you turn away from me, deliberately casting your eyes in another direction, then my utterance is not defined as a greeting, but perhaps as a cheep attempt to gloss over a rent in our relationship. In the same way, I can't give you help unless you treat it as help. The meaning of what I say, then, depends on collaborative action (coaction): not on what I say or what you say, but on the *relationship* between our sayings. Consider the following four interchanges between two coworkers, Steve and Marsha, as she passes him in the hall one day:

Steve: Hey Marsha, I really do like that dress.

Marsha: [playfully] You should be a fashion designer. Great taste!

Steve: Hey Marsha, I really do like that dress.

Marsha: [twinkle in her eye] You look pretty cute yourself today.

Steve: Hey Marsha, I really do like that dress.

Marsha: [frowns] One more word out'a you, and I'll report you for harassment.

Steve: Hey Marsha, I really do like that dress.

Marsha: [smiles] You should see what's underneath!

Who then is Steve? What is kind of person is he? Perceptive, charming, aggressive, or sexy? Much depends on Marsha, whose reply creates his personality.

Now consider the possibility that what we say about our states of mind—our thoughts, feelings, beliefs, and so on—is not located "in the head" so much as in the unfolding conversation. Here is a conversation between friends:

Shirley: I'm really depressed, nothing is coming out right in my work, I just seem to give so many hours to it, and it seems worthless.

Rebecca: I can really understand how you feel. I've been in those situations before.

Shirley: I don't know what I am going to do. I've got to get a grip, and I don't like to take drugs.

In effect, Rebecca joins in creating the reality of the depression, and as a result of her defining herself as depressed, Shirley sets out to find a solution. Let's try a variation:

Shirley: I'm really depressed, nothing is coming out right in my work, I just seem to give so many hours to it, and it seems worthless.

Rebecca: You know, I don't really think you're depressed. You haven't slept in two nights, and I just think you are terribly tired.

Shirley: Yeah, I really need to get more sleep. Reminds me of the joke about the guy who thought he was depressed for a whole year, and then realized he was just bored.

Joining with Rebecca's reply, Shirley may now simply get more sleep. A third possibility:

Shirley: I'm really depressed, nothing is coming out right in my work, I just seem to give so many hours to it, and it seems worthless.

Rebecca: You know, you do depression better than almost anyone I ever knew. It's a dramatic tour de force, just makes your audience want to weep.

Shirley: [laughs] Yeah, I guess I am a little overdramatic . . .

Of course, Rebecca takes chances by turning Shirley's expression into a performance. Shirley could respond with irritation, thus negating Rebecca. Whether Rebecca is depressed, then, is altogether dependent on the unfolding of the conversation. Yet, while conversation is fluid, it is also constrained. The discourse of the mind is lodged in tradition, and these traditions also include the way in which conversations unfold. In other words, one could not legitimately have an emotion outside a relational process.

Does this sound odd? Consider first the possibility of having an emotion that is all one's own, born within:

Frank: I am angry as hell.
Richard: Why, Frank, what happened . . .
Frank: Nothing happened, I just feel angry as hell, that's all . . .

By Western conventions, Frank is a very strange creature. If he went about town expressing his anger for no particular reason he would soon be locked away. But let's say Frank provides an answer. Consider the following possibilities:

Someone stole the dirt off my front tires;
Someone took a close look at my tires;
Someone thought my tires might be new;
Someone stole my tires.

From a Western standpoint, only the final reason for anger would make sense. It is not simply that we cannot sensibly have an emotion without a reason outside the emotion itself, but the reason for the emotion must also be socially acceptable. Now let us expand: if you express anger to a friend, and you can offer an acceptable reason, then the friend has limited possibilities for action. He or she cannot simply turn and walk away, or fall on the floor in giggles. Such actions would make no sense as appropriate responses to an expression of anger. However, by conventional standards, any of the following would be legitimate:

Expressions of sympathy;
Curiosity about how it happened;
Reminiscing about a similar experience.

Each of these responses would also function to legitimate the "fact" of your anger. In effect, your anger only makes sense within a sequence of actions. I like to call these *relational scenarios*. In this sense, the emotion of anger is only one component in a recognizable scenario. All the components are required to bring anger into a reality. Emotions belong neither to you nor me, but to our participation in a cultural tradition.

At the same time, we are not obliged to follow such traditions. They are only conventions, and conventions are open to transformation. Together we can mold new futures. For change agents in society—therapists, social workers, educators, conflict reduction professionals, and the like—this fact presents a creative challenge. Many of our traditional scenarios are inimical to our well-being.

When Mary and I work with therapists we often present them with common, but debilitating scenarios and ask them to create alternative lines. What could be said differently and when? What new and more hopeful lines could be inserted into the mix? These we subsequently act out, to explore how fitting and potentially effective the suggestions are. The following is a scenario that we use to illustrate escalating anger between a husband and wife, just the kind of escalation that often culminates in family violence.

Mike is sprawled before the TV, beer in hand, watching a football game. Mali enters:

Mali: The American Express bill came today. You charged over $400 for that dinner you had with your old buddy, Frank! What kind of restaurant was that? The Pink Pussycat? Is that one of those "gentleman's clubs"? I don't work hard everyday so you can throw it away on booze and women.

Mike: Forgettabout it, Mali . . . I didn't see Frank for a long time; he was in the army, you know . . . So get off my case!

Mali: Oh yeah . . . easy come, easy go huh . . . I can't stand that attitude . . . that you would just waste money like that, throwing it away . . . burning it up, I mean I'm up to here with your . . .

Mike: Little Miss Righteousness, huh . . . Look at you . . . You spend twice that much for a dress . . . And what about all that makeup, and god, when I think of what you put into shoes . . . Hell, I'll go out and drink with my buddies whenever and wherever I want . . .

Mali: Look Mr. Big Spender, I work hard . . . I need everything I buy . . . It's my money . . . So get off this macho shtick . . .

Mike: What you make is shit . . . I'm the one who brings in the real bucks.

Mali: Yeah . . . You make some money . . . but where did you get that job? From my father. Without my family you would be a worthless slug . . . stuck somewhere down a gutter.

Mike: [now yelling] Your family! I've had that Asian Mafia up to here . . . so damn controlling . . . And you're just like'em . . .

Mali: [shrieking] Go to hell, you lousy . . .

Mike: . . . [he starts to strike Mali]

Our audiences have come up with many very creative insertions into this escalation of animosity. These can wait for another book. But the optimistic outcome is that if the mental world is essentially a world of relational performance, and this world is of our creation, then we may create new and more promising futures.

11

Performing Theory

Mary Gergen

It was 1988, and I was a fellow at the Netherlands Institute for Advanced Study. In my lovely study, spacious and elegant, with carpets, oil paintings, and a garden view, I experienced the contentment that Virginia Woolf must have envisioned with her notion of a room of one's own (and a satisfactory stipend). My conversational partner and soul mate was missing, gone to Heidelberg to fulfill his Humboldt scholarship duties, and so when I became aroused by the sexist implications of an academic piece (about which you will find out below) I vented my spleen into my computer. The result became a performance playlet, an imaginary conversation between two women, and finally the offending man, in three acts. I did not write this piece to pay a gas bill (as poet Robert Frost cautioned against); I did it because of the delicious feeling of free expression. Without the critical eyes of academic tradition at my shoulder, I could dramatize the tensions I experienced between being favorable to postmodern ideas, as a feminist, and yet being offended by the totally masculine world that was invoked by the author in question.

Later, a "gas bill" arrived in the form of an invitation to present at a conference on postmodernism at Aarhus University in Denmark. I prepared not only by rehearsing my play, but also by considering my appearance as the actor of my piece. To emphasize my femininity, I purchased a ten-foot-long red boa and wore high heels, makeup, and jewelry. No hiding behind the podium, disembodying, and disappearing for me. I enlisted John Shotter, a friend and colleague, to read the man's voice. The performance went off as planned, and afterwards, many women in the audience clustered around me. Something in what I did created a connection with them, even though it was in English and hard to follow, even for me. When a special issue of a journal with papers from the conference was planned, my presentation was rejected. Through some arm-twisting from Ken Gergen, and his refusal to allow his paper to be published if mine was not, the editor relented. Later, the compilation was made into a book in which the editor and conference host praised my contribution as a postmodern gem.[1] How vindicated I felt, and how inspiring to continue in the performative vein.

To conclude, I sent the manuscript to Stephen Tyler, whose work had triggered the outburst. He responded by saying he enjoyed it immensely and gave it to his class to read. Good guy!

AGAINST MOD MASCU-LINITY AND POST-MOD MACHO: A FEMINIST END-PLAY

Let's begin with a scare tactic: what we've all been on the edge of our seats to bring up and to deny. Face to face, can we stare it down? Will it get us down?

Has the end of history come? Nothing left but to demystify and deconstruct the illusory claims to knowledge made by the long track of wise men stretching from now to once upon a time. The task is to unmask. To rid the world of the pretense behind the propositions—demonstrating knowledge makers as fools after all. Nothing will be left, a charred shell, a burnt out book, a leveled plain. Then the ending comes: he "beholds the world blankly, with a knowingness that dissolves feeling and commitment into irony" (or so said Todd Gitlin in 1988). And do we take it lie-ing down? Do we disappear?

Although there is much to be said about critical unmasking, the present text advocates a feminist a-version to this as the end game. Does it all come down to this? I don't think so. Yet, in a postmodern-feminist moment, I am on this side, and often simultaneously repelled. Feminists cannot hold the deconstructive posture (it makes us tense, and often past, at that). We long for movement. And in our dance, as postmodern mimes, we might just renovate, restore, and refurnish the social sciences. Faithfully faithless, we can play with the context, but not lose our way in the motion. As Marilyn Strathern notes, we can employ ironic gestures, in a "deliberate juxtaposition of contexts, pastiche perhaps, but no jumble" (1987, 268).

It is within such a postmodernist moment that this piece is set. The script that follows was originally designed as a dramatic reading. It is intentionally not "straight talk" and often difficult to follow. The reasons for this shift in linguistic styling are several and significant. First, as feminist postmodernists have come to realize, most of the forms of intelligible discourse in Western culture are suffused with androcentric biases (Butler 1990; Crawford 1995; Gergen 1991; Heilbrun 1988; Lather 1995). Grammar, logic, and narrative structures, for example, lend themselves to certain problematic ends (such as hierarchy and separation). For feminists such as Luce Irigaray (1985), Julia Kristeva (1984), and Patti Lather (1995) the conclusion argues for a breaking with the prevailing traditions of discourse. With Mary Daly (1978) on our side, we can slip into bewitchery.

Second, to adopt the customary forms of "straight talk" is, for the postmodern, to invite the reader again into the cul-de-sac of traditionalism—that is, into the belief that language maps the terrain. In order to avoid such objectification, one is invited to play with the traditions, unsettle the words, so that the consciousness that the postmodern's language is itself subject to deconstruction is never lost (St. Pierre 1997). Finally, from the postmodern standpoint, "straight talk" restricts the signifiers (or the meaning of words) in arbitrary ways, which may pass unnoticed. For the postmodernists, social science writing should, in principle, be shaken loose from its authorized source. The language should be liberated and allowed to rove more evocatively.

The immediate inspiration for this refrain (he might say, the target) was a plenary address at the Conference on Critical Anthropology at the University of Amsterdam given in December 1988 by Stephen Tyler, professor of Anthropology at Rice University and a leading hot-rodder in the postmodern turn.[2] Freed from the boundaries of convention, alert to linguistic snares, Tyler pursues a course that roams helter-skelter over those left, disciplined-bound, behind. My text is a reaction to the solitary stance (t)he(y) take(s). A lament couched in ironic teasing, as well as an angry chastisement of his text, my writing resounds as a yelp of the Big Bear against her errant sons and against all those who assume ontological freedom, transitivity, and solipsistic solitude; it is addressed to those who proclaim the immediacy of one/two/selfness—of separation and dissolution—and who revel in a phallic superfluidity that denies connections, relationships, and the possibility of love.

Stage Directions

Setting for the Original Performance

A typical academic auditorium in darkness, with bright lights illuminating the stage. A podium is set upon a desk, which may be used or not by the reader as a chair, table, or stand. An overhead projector screen is illuminated behind the area stage left of the desk where the words are projected as they are spoken.

Characters

First woman, a feminist postmodern critic.
Second woman, her companion.
PM [or postmodern] man

Costume

Black turtleneck, pants, and heels (optional). One and a half meters of red feather boa flung about the shoulders and neck. A hand mirror with a broken glass, face out, is strung on a ribbon or string about the neck as a necklace.

Script Notes

The performance is in two parts; (metaphorically) it is a pie, a seafood crepe, an empinada, or perhaps a pregnant woman. Part I is the crust; Part II is the filling. The designation of [ ] indicate stage directions. The performer may use "finger snaps" to indicate quotation marks for the audience. The prologue of the performance is composed of the introductory lines from Tyler's "Post-Modern Ethnography" (1986). It describes Tyler's two mental selves, his mind as the book and his mind as the word processor/computer.

The Performance

Prologue

Tyler: . . . I'm of two minds about this . . . the unmoved one and the moving continuum, Apollo and Dionysus . . . the mind as a book . . . a passionate attention that . . . joins life and experience in an act of production/reproduction/creativity, a conceit that we call the concept . . . and thus note the role of Eros in the sexual act of conceiving the concept, the perfection of form, the fixed entity of the idea, the achieved whole of the inner psyche that makes the integrity of the private mind and repeats itself in the solitude of the book, in the trance-like stasis of reading and writing.
   . . . my other mind . . . the mind of the word processor/computer . . . replaces the steadiness of contemplative formulation with an excess of dynamic possibilities, turning my private solitude into the public network, destroying my authorship by making a totalized textuality in which the text is only ancillary.

Part I: The Crust

First woman: Mille Feuille for the Fruits de Mer. How to make sense of the senses to follow. How many sheets can we layer, to make "womb" for the filling to fit? A winding sheet around the carcass of words.

Second woman: [aside] It would be much easier (and more to the point) to talk about hot dogs and hot dog buns.

First woman: But much less elegant, and much less French. The problem . . . my problem: How to compos(t)e a postmodernist pose, one that does not crush my feminist folds?

Second woman: Irigaray speaks of the folds of femininity in perpetual embrace. As women, in a constant caress, caressing ourselves, and maybe each other.

First woman: No wonder we do not come to the point the way men claim to do! My question: Can there be a Re-Union with Difference? Is it possible to conceive of A FEMINIST POSTMODERN/POSTMODERN FEMINIST FEMME/ POSTMODERN MODIFIED/??

Second woman: Let's say yes, but it's a High Anxiety situation. There is much to criticize, and I've done my share. Donna Haraway said it with in-tension: "The further I get in describing . . . postmodernism . . . the more nervous I get. The imagery of . . . high-tech military fields . . . where blips of light called players disintegrate (what a metaphor!) each other in order to stay in the knowledge and power game" (1988, 577).

First woman: Where does the ray-a-thon become a rhoda-thon? Is this another squeeze play? And we're still the marginal mayo and mustard?

Second woman: Craig Owens noticed it too: "Few women have engaged in the modernism/postmodernism debate . . . Postmodernism may be another masculine invention engineered to exclude women" (1983, 61).

First woman: If he says it, can my intuition be totally untracked?

Second woman: My dream would be a wedlock not a deadlock. To have the best of both worlds, and leave the modern one behind. To throw a curve ball, that knots the haves and the have-nots into a spinning wheel of dense desire.

First woman: Whose desire? That's another course to pursue. Teresa De Lauretis speaks of a story as a question of desire. "But whose desire is it that speaks, and whom does that desire address?" (1984, 113). Is it unreal to imagine:

Letting go of	taking	and	combining
Modernist	Postmod		Feminist
stability	partiality		connection
linearity	playfulness		construction
control/manipulation	pastiche		commitment
polar opposites	parody		dialogue
"real world"	difference		politics

Second woman: As Edward Said said: "Transform binary opposition into an economy in which terms circulate" (1983, 155). Or as a chaoticist might insist—let the boiling pot of words break the liminarity and the clarity of orderly flow. Uncongeal categories, Both and And.

"Have your cake and eat it"—two. (There's a Mariann'ette, French again, a puppet game for you and me. Let us probe for the Unsaid.)

First woman: Postmodernism . . . Is it just another sport to add to the Academic Olympics? Who can deconstruct the fastest and the mostest? Bring on the muscle men, and let them strain. Steroid doses and noselogic poses. GOLD /SILVER/BRONZE [she sings a phrase of *La Marseillaise*] "Allons enfants de la patrie" . . . [pause]

Second woman: Did anybody say anything about anyone who wasn't playing their game?

First woman: There was some mention of women, at least of their bodies. They're the supplement, the ex-centrics. Without phALL- USes they can't go very far, especially in this game.

Second woman: Nobody seemed to notice that all the players are "IN" the establishment. From the Sorbonne to Santa Cruz, the same old tricks, ruses, disguises, they use them to kick the OLD GUARD OUT of power. Re-Volving door policy—So that they could be INNER. More IN, less OUT. They won't hold a door open for anyone. Just the same old "Sexual politics" (the old IN and OUT).

First woman: Well, that's what got me going! It's a love/hate relationship—postmodernism/feminism/how perfectly PM/PMS. Their endless discourses colliding in one condrumatic phrase. But two isms don't make an are, or do they?

Second woman:	Collapsing the opposition of love and hate. Collapsing the opposition: femme and them, me and he.
First woman:	Collapsing the opposition (by taking the wind out of their sails?). Co-LAP-SING the (T)OP-POSition. (All missionaries are being recalled for faulty transmissions.) Or is it "Co-Lapsinging"—a name for conjoining. Let our laps sing together . . . Much better.
Second woman:	No one needs to be "on top." We don't have to listen to what those dick-shunaries told us.
First woman:	Then let's start a deconstruction. It can happen anywhere. How about here? Perhaps the Zen master is right. It all/nothing makes sense.
Second woman:	A word about Stephen Tyler to whom this piece is daddy-kated. He's a cover boy (do you think I'm covering something up?), an undercover (anthro)agent; looking to discover; running for cover. But there are no more hiding places. It's all on the surface, now. Nothing can hide under pre-texts any more.
First woman:	Tyler is a PM magician . . . talks and even writes PM-ese. Read *The Unspeakable* if you don't believe me. I admire him. Yet he is the target. I am after the pack. He is the random one whose number came up. My ode is to and with and through him. In the intertextuality of things, he is a woof and I am a Whorf. Now I shall spin us together in a centrifuge of text. Come follow me along, over and under we go, shuttles on the shades of weaving words.

Part II: The Filling

PM man:	All I ever wanted to do was to stay in my room and "play with IT."
First woman:	Behold. S.T. one in a new chain of linguistic magistics . . . U.V.W.X.Y.Z. The end of the line . . . where we all have to get off now. How to "get off," ah, there's the rub. It's nobler in the minds of men perhaps, but is that enough? That is also the question. The PM Man, torn apart . . . full of contra-DICK-shun. Of two minds . . . Platonist, left hemispheric, the "ur-form of the scribal hand" . . . "taking in hand" . . . E-Man-cipate . . . "UNMOVED," AND the other mind, Dionysian, the anticipate "MOVED"? Yes, why not? We were brought up on opposition. "Moved . . . E-Moved . . . E-MOTION" . . .

Second woman:	Emotion . . . Now we get to the heart of the matter.
First woman:	Sorry to disappoint you, but it's a wrong spelling; don't forget the hyphen. It's E (hyphen) Motion. His motion is not from the heart; it's from the hardware.
PM man:	Give me SPACE! Keep it all separate. That's where it's comFORTable. (One Man, One FORT!) E-MOTION . . . the "moving continuum." E-Motion on the screen. "The mind of the word processor/computer . . . poke at . . . mon-key." (Get the French connection? It's all in the tongue.) Losing the self-consciousness of the left brain, peeling down the cortex to the electronic core . . . fingering "mon" key, the magic wand that opens doors, boxes, hidden files . . . mesmerized by the flickering shadow images, dancing naked on the screen . . .
First woman:	He's CELL-Eee-Brate-ing alone, total-(itarian)-ly in "calculative power, total manipulative control, abundant resource, speed, complete management . . . hypnotized by the phosphorescent glow of moving symbols" . . . Listen to him hum.
PM man:	[shouting] "Power is mine!" . . . "I have the instantaneous and total knowledge of god and am ONE with the movement of thought . . . I AM THE MOVING MATRIX!! . . . "
First woman:	CLIMAX, cut, end of paragraph . . . CURTAIN.
Second woman:	[softly] Should we pull the shades? Cigarette?
PM man:	[tired] It is dawn by now. No one can see in. Everyone is asleep. Besides we are not ashamed. We are scholars. It's the thing now. Left or Right: The Thing Was Always It.
First woman:	PM, Poor Man, just trying to get his head together. Or heads together? Is a Man of two heads or three? It's a trinity . . . three in one . . . indivisible . . . a miracle, the priest said. We should all respect it, even if we can't understand.
Second woman:	And be forgiven if we envy. (Who will forgive us? Our Sigmund who art in heaven?)
First woman:	But it's no fun when they won't let you play. Or when all you can be is the nurse, or the patient, or the ground they measure and inspect. Always peeking; then they say, "Is that all there is?" When will they learn? [forceful] Don't mess with Mother Nature!

Second woman: E-movement . . . B-movement . . . Re-movement. "When the boys came out to play, Georgie Porgie ran away."

First woman: Who are they trying to scare off? Full of Power and Manipulative Control, Abundant Resources, Speed, Complete Management. The New Army, complete with portable Zenises. Pulling the rug out from under the OLD GUARD. (Didn't we all want to run out of the stands and CHEER!!!?) Down with the OLD ORDER . . . Foundations of Modernity, split into Gravity's Rainbow/Rules shredded, ribbons adorning the May POLE, wavering in the Breeze of breathtaking words/ABSOLUTE-ly nothinged by the shocking PM tropes/smashing icons with

iron(ic)s/Wreaking CON-SENSE
with NON-SENSE/PARODYING
PARADING
PANDERING
PARADOXING
PLAYING
POUNDING
PRIMPING
PUMPING

What fun! [singing] " . . . London Bridges Falling Down [then shouting] (DE-CONSTRUCT-ED) [resume singing] MY FAIR LADY." Where can WE jump in? Shall we twirl your batons? Can we all form a circle? Dance around the fire? The Pole? The falling bridges? Give us a hand. Give us a hand? Give us a hand . . .

PM man: All they ever want are hand-outs . . . Give 'em an inch they'll take a mile. How many inches do they think we've got? [a brief pause, then, addressing Women] Besides can't you see we've got play to do? It's not easy just going off to play each day. It takes practice . . . dedication . . . grace. It's not something you can just join in like that. We've got our formation. Can't you see you'll just muck it up? We're in the wrecking business. What business is that of yours? "You make, we break": we can write it on the truck. Next thing you'll want us to settle down and play house. We've

	got to be movin' on. It's part of the code. Girls can't be in combat. Besides John Wayne doesn't talk to them, so adios. Don't call us, we'll call you.
First woman:	That call has a familiar ring to it. The call of the WILD.
PM man:	We aren't animals; and don't call us an army! Better a merry dis-band-ment of (dis) Con-victors;

(dis) Con-artists; (dis)co-dandies;
(dis)iden-ticals; (dis)-sent-uals;
(dis)-coursers; (dis)i-paters;
(dis)contents; (dis)-ap-pere-ers . . .
        (Dig that French)
  cr
    ac
      king
        up (by any meaning you like)
      c
    rac
  king
up (whatever other meaning(s) you like) . . . THE JOINT

First woman:	How many joints you got in mind?
PM man:	Hey, it's not personal. No hard feelings?
First woman:	"How do you mean that?"
Second woman:	Makes you wonder if she has a "double entendre" in mind. Those Frenchies are at it again.
PM man:	If you wanna make an omelette, you gotta break some eggs.
First woman:	But we've got the eggs.
PM man:	Which comes first, the chicks or the eggs? Sorry, I couldn't help it. Old gag line, part of the new PM ritual: Say whatever comes into your head, especially if it's a dumb "yoke." [laughs at his own joke]
First woman:	Which head?
Second woman:	Another double entendre?!
PM man:	One for all and all for one. At least for the moment. That's another thing. We don't make promises. Just another word for COMMITMENT (the really big C-word, the one that gets you behind bars, and I don't mean mixing martinis). A rolling stone gathers no moss and no mille-deux.
First woman:	Mick Jagger has children.

PM man:	Babies are phallic. If you need one, get one.
First woman:	But your phallus doesn't need bread.
PM man:	"Let them eat cake," as good ol' Marie put it. She had a feel for our rap.
First woman:	That doesn't solve the problem.
PM man:	It's not my problem. Postmodern life is, as Deleuze sez, nomadic. And S.T. added, "We are all homeless wanderers on the featureless, post-industrial steppe, tentless nomads, home packed up." And as a NATO tank commander once said, "You can't have an army when you gotta bring along the outhouse for the dames."
First woman:	Looks like it's going to be a short revolution—about one generation.
PM man:	Au contraire, Baby, we've just begun. I mean, the trashing is in dis-progress. Disciplines to dismantle/Methods to maul/Truth to trample/Origins to emasculate.
First woman:	Who's on the clean-up committee?
PM man:	You sound like somebody's mother. Whose side are you on anyway? Few minutes ago you wanted to dance in the streets. Down with the old, up with the new. (Never satisfied; always want what ya can't get. Bitch, bitch, bitch.)
First woman:	You sound de-fence-ive. Have I got your goat?
PM man:	Now you're getting down to something. Thanks, but no thanks. I get off graphically. Who needs flesh. And I can logoff any time any time any time . . . Let's leave it at that. Stephen Tyler has said: Postmodernism accepts the paradoxical CONsequences of . . . irreconcilable ambiguity without attempting to end the CONflict by imposing CLOSURE . . . We're a-dispersing . . . "dispursing" . . . we are getting further and further away. Space is beautiful.
First woman:	It's gonna be mighty COLD out there . . .
PM man:	Earthling, do you read me? . . . do you read me?? . . . do you . . . reeeeead . . . ???
First woman:	You're fading, Major Tom.
	The signal is getting weaker and weaker. It is running out in space. It is running out of space . . .

[SILENCE]

12

Theatrical Power

Mary Gergen

The inspiration for this piece came from a growing sense as I aged that, as an older woman, I had begun to disappear. Unlike when I was younger, I had the sense now that the eyes that observed me would turn away, as though they had caught a glimpse of an ordinary tree. This could be considered comfortable, in that there is also a sense of safety in the oblivion. No one is going to intrude on your privacy, leer, or make sexy or unkind remarks. No one is going to move in too close or pinch your butt. At the same time, there is also a sense that you're being discounted or have become invisible. Your actions don't count anymore. In a sense, older women are victimized by ordinary social interchange, invited to accept their being redundant, their having little to offer in the social sphere. They collaborate in the disappearing act. What other options do they have, but to "age gracefully." Some women protest or act with a certain willingness to swim against the current (Cole and Gergen 2012). This piece was created to celebrate this possibility and offer a role model. I decided that my words would have to be accompanied by strong actions in order to emphasize that both actions and words must be combined to create social change. Originally, I performed this at the national meeting of the American Psychological Association, where I did a strip tease, which concluded with the removal of my stockings, shoes, gloves, and raincoat. I did not go beyond this, but after this initial offering, I left the stockings at home. (Taking off panty hose in public requires training that I never had.)

Woman as Spectacle, or Facing Off: Cavorting with Carn-ival Knowledge

This is me, as I am here, as I am pictured. It is important that I am gaspingly noticeable. I attract attention. The attention is not altogether admiring. In fact, it is shocking to many in the audience that a woman past fifty would wear such colors, in such combinations, with sexual overtones in her demeanor and garments, engaging in mildly impolite activities, such as chewing gum, swigging brandy from a flask, carrying a cigar, telling jokes. I call myself POMO, a play on postmodern, and Mama, and other things.

The second title, *Facing Off: Cavorting with Carn-ival Knowledge*, which I have used on occasion, suggests the process of losing face, that is, of discarding the mask of propriety, which I am doing in my performance. At the same time, "facing off" is a hockey term, used when

two players of opposite teams face each other and vie for the puck through their stick handling. Facing off suggests an aggressive posture, and can be stretched metaphorically to include standing up for one's right to reveal a self beyond the constraints of social propriety. Cavorting—having fun, moving about in a playful manner, is always an important part of any performative occasion. Carn-ival is a play on *carne*, meat, my meat in particular—the body as flesh—and "ival," or evil—the body contrasted with the spirit. Carnival can also be read as a totality, the festival in which good and evil are transposed. Carnival, as Michael Bakhtin has described it, treasures the ambiguity and the transgressive potentials of the charade, and yet, in an ironic twist, upheavals such as carnival are sanctioned by the ruling bodies, and this act of acceptance ultimately reinstates their own power (Bakhtin 1981). We cannot so easily escape the place society has "meted" out for us.

As the house lights dim, and the spotlight falls upon me, I begin:

Act I: Stripping Down to Basics

[*Chewing gum, blowing bubbles, takes the gum out and places it somewhere convenient, but impolite*]

How I love an audience. What a place for a starstruck kid. Kid, I said. Do I hear some snickering? "Who is she kidding? She's more like an old goat than a starstruck kid."

[*Takes off hat and gloves. Sets down a gold lame purse full of things to eat and drink and smoke, perhaps*]

In March 1998 Beatrice Wood, the Mama of Dada, died in her studio in California, just days after she gave a party in honor of the director of the movie *Titanic*. The obituary said she was one hundred five, but she quarreled with the calculation. She always said that if scientists have showed that time is relative, then she was thirty-two. The secret to a long life depended on two things, she said: chocolate and young men. (Not much to disagree with there, although what means young? And maybe men aren't the only choice, but otherwise Beatrice was right on.) Let's dedicate this performance to the Mama of Dada, may her spirit live forever.

Age is a social construction. So, like Beatrice, I'm somewhere between six and sixty today, depending on how we get along together. We'll see.

Regardless of whatever age I am, this is a pretty formidable place to be standing, given that some of you have other expectations about how a proper woman (and professor) should behave. It's a tough balancing act . . . to do what I do in such sacred territory. But, I'll give it a whirl.

[Swirling about with arms out]
[Taking a slug of brandy from a silver flask. It is real brandy]
Ah, just a drop of "Kool-Aid" to get the juices flowing.
I'm warming up.
[Taking off the cape]

But before I get too far along, let me just thank you for coming, and joining in our conversation. You make a girl's day. That is what this relational stuff is all about. I couldn't be standing up here without you. And, of course, if you are wondering how come you are listening to me, and watching me, and puzzling out what I'm up to, then you just better reflect back and consider what you did to deserve me. Cause I certainly didn't make this up all by myself.

But you might ask: "What is this 'Woman as Spectacle' thing all about? What is she going to do? And why?"

Here I am . . . a nice girl from Lake Wobegon, looking like a raspberry tart, and we ain't celebrating Marti Gras just yet. What's the psychology of being outlandish? . . .Outside the customs, peculiar . . . provocative . . . verging on the weird, the grotesque, the carnivalesque. A woman on the edge of feminine respectability . . . or way over the line.

One thing is for sure. I'm here to amuse you . . . and bemuse you . . . even confuse you. All those ooze words . . . is that sexy or what?

[Pointing to a corner of the stage] Over there is an imaginary circle of my textual friends. My social ghosts, I call them. One of them, Mary Russo, has charted the dangers of what I attempt: "Making a spectacle out of oneself seem[s] a specifically feminine danger. The danger . . . of an exposure . . . Women who make spectacles of themselves have done something wrong, have stepped, as it were, into the limelight out of turn—too young or too old, too early or too late—and yet anyone, any woman, can make a spectacle out of herself if she is not careful" (1986, 213).

[Addressing the audience]

WHAT IS THE WORST SPECTACLE YOU EVER MADE OF YOURSELF? Arguing with somebody more important than you in public? Belching, or God Forbid, farting in company, or even alone? Getting caught eating like you were hungry? Being rude to somebody, even if he was molesting you?

DO YOUR CHEEKS BURN TO THINK OF IT? EVERYONE WHISPERING BEHIND YOUR BACK . . . HOW EMBARRASSING! . . . IF ONLY YOU COULD DISAPPEAR INTO THIN AIR (IF ONLY I HAD NOT BROUGHT IT UP)!

[Pause, pointing to the corner]

Peggy Penn, over there in my magic circle, has spelled out one of those moments in a poem called "Omen for Women." Here are her lines:

> At twelve my russet blood rolled out,
> everyone on the bus to Latrobe, PA.
> whispered, See, her eggs are multiplying!
> her insides sloughing off! See! It's dripping on her knees!

It ain't been called the Curse for nothing.
Is there no recourse but to relive our endless anguishes?
Peggy's no Pollyanna, but she saves herself from humiliation in the final lines of this poem:

> Leaving a trail
> for you to find me in eleven years.

(There's a positive spin if I've ever seen one. Hansel and Gretel for the pubescent set. Follow my droplets and you'll find your way home.)

COULD YOUR SPECTACLE EVER BE REVALUED? MIGHT THERE BE SOMETHING TO SALVAGE IN YOUR STORY? EVEN POLITICAL POTENTIAL? (Or is this feminist jive?)

Mary Russo also said: " In contemplating these dangers, I grew to admire . . . the lewd, exuberant . . . Mae West . . . Her bold affirmations of feminine performance, imposture, and masquerade . . . suggest cultural politics for women." Wasn't her line, "Is that a banana in your pocket or are you just glad to see me?" (Russo 1986, 213).

bell hooks—I admire her outlandish starlight—concurs in her rap about African American women: "When we give expression . . . to those aspects of our identity forged in marginality, we may be seen as 'spectacle.' Yet . . . this is a risk we must run . . . it is a means by which culture is transformed and not simply reproduced with different players in the same game" (hooks 1990, 154).

Transformation, re-creation, even recreation, the politics of fun. Let us move from living with fear, the most elegant weapon, as artist Jenny Holzer's neon sign proclaims, to a raucous appreciation of our right to be. And to be in violations of the codes by which we are told to live.

If we want to strip away the bars holding us in place, the corset stays of respectability, and tease the audience with our unbounded flesh, how shall we begin?

[Taking off some clothes . . . in some performances stockings, in others a boa or a jacket; or putting one leg up on a chair to check stocking seams]

We walk a thin line in this little strip tease . . . slathering the seams of sentences so they all run soothingly into one; smoothing out the ragged edges that might catch us up. Snag our hemlines . . . Stub our toes, or sliver our heels on the runways of our stage of life.

Beryl Curt warns that "such words [should] . . . always arouse suspicion. Their very ease . . . beguiles the [listener] . . . into believing they are merely mirroring the world 'as it really is,' and obscures their ability to glamour that reality into being" (1994, 14).

I am guilty. I do wish to glamour a reality into being, preening these words into worlds. You have been forewarned.

[Waving her magic wand]

The spectacle under construction: needs more introduction. Over there *[pointing to another part of the stage]* are people who would want to strip me of my style. At my age (chronological that is) I am meant to disappear. I should have been gone long ago. In the dance of the life cycle, I am being propelled against the wall. *[Moving backwards as though being pushed from the front, arms extended, curled in the middle]* Centrifugal forces spin me to the chairs, from which I rose so long ago . . . arms that circled me, and kept me on the floor. Oh, how I could dance. *[Doing a bit of a cha cha cha]*

[Taking up a sheer purple scarf that is tucked into the purse] Now they've let me go. My dance card is empty. *[Placing the large scarf over her head, covering her face]* Now, I'm melding with the walls. Pressing into paper . . . melting with the glue . . . Stuck, not pinned and wriggling like Eliot's Prufrock, but misting into mottled lavender, without a muscle's twitch. *[Standing with arms out, covered by the veil of purple]* This is the fate woman of a mature age. *[Removing scarf, keeping it in hand]* She is somewhere over forty and, according to some, about as useful as a fruit fly (at least they have the courtesy to die swiftly when their breeding days are done). If she cannot procreate she is lifeless you see, but not dead. She never should attract attention. She learns to be the anti-spectacle. Yet she is the object of our gaze.

Such hatred we sometimes feel for her. *[Wringing scarf like a neck]* That shameful blot on the image of our youth. Couldn't we just wring her neck? Be done with her. No one needs her . . . hoarder of Medicare . . . Social Security sadsack . . . our tax dollars feeding a body no one wants to see.

But lest we discard her so quickly, she is also me, and perhaps you. She is our destiny, those of the female persuasion. Ugghhh, should we call for our pills, ply ourselves with hormones? Slather on our creams? Invite the knife to cut into our own throats, and pay for that pleasure? *[Making slitting gestures]*

Or shall we tipple into our drugs of sweet forgetting? *[Taking another brandy sip]*

Is there anyone to call? Will 911 give us any help?

Today she is the creature under construction. And I, in my spectacular role, a Postmodern Mama, with nothing to lose but my invisibility. I challenge those who would erase these fine lines. *[Motioning over her body]*

Act II: Faces Off

On the face of it, its a challenging task. How do we claim a space on the floor when we are told that the music has stopped? How can we face up to this rejection? It is a challenging task.

Let's play on words of faces . . . on the face of it . . . face values, those of sameness, of identities, of what identities are worth. Facing off . . . challenging the status quo . . . taking off identities . . . losing one's face . . . losing face, the name of shame . . . but this time . . . how can we do it without dread?

We spin over possibilities . . . questioning identities, selfhoods, the singles of selves. Poised for the face off, we lose who we are.

The face becomes the mask . . . masking the face . . . facing our masks. Who else can we become?

Is this only a Midsummer Night's Dream? We struggle for meaning and mistaken identity. In this struggle for meaning, can we ring up a hat trick? Pull the rabbit out of the hat? Change her luck?

Or in the moments of spectacle will we be defaced?

Or are we off sides here? Betraying one's own . . . a feminist involved in the postmod game . . . losing one's self in the flux of the game. Playing with the dialogic. Giving up or losing one's place . . . Shimmering and shaking we shuck our old selves.

In this masquerade where parody is paramount we must fake it as we go. Well, at least we have some talent and experience there. In the politics of spectacle, we will reclaim a space.

[Pause]

[Pointing to an aisle seat]

The man on the aisle is trying to understand what all the fuss is about. Why are we men accused? Why blame us if we are swayed by the beauty of youth. We are mere animals, after all. Yearning to spread our seeds abroad. Who can quarrel with the dictates of fate? Sooner or later we are all victims of the game. Nature's call is wild. It's not political, it's biological.

In the dominant world of science, support for the gentleman endures. Doctor Freud had this to say: "A man of about thirty seems youthful . . . A woman of about the same age frequently staggers us by her psychological rigidity . . . There are no paths open to her for further development" (1933, 134).

Sociobiologists are crawling out from under every rock, claiming that our fates are in our genes, and they ain't talking Levis.

As evolutionary psychologist David Buss, has said, "All around the world men are more interested in the youth and beauty of their sexual partners and less discriminating in their choice of partners than women are" (1995, 155).

So be it?

We hear feminist researchers lament the discourse of science on our wall-flower women: "Images of disease and deficiency . . . become the basis of discourse about women's lives in general"; "Every woman over fifty years of age becomes a patient." The disease, of course, is menopause. *[Taking out a fan]* I always say the best treatment, next to chocolate and young men, is a fan. "The characterization of women as different and pathological . . . tends to provide a . . . justification for misogyny in the wider culture . . . It is basically a political phenomenon disguised as medical science."

Egglets and Wigglets—the whole world reduced to microscopic protoplasmic difference. And "The Whigs" have it.

I will not wait for Science to come to its senses. We haven't got all day. We must deface its smug veneer. Graffiti its granting agencies. Pull the plug on its polemics.

Yet, how is it possible?

It is dangerous business to mess with the master's discourse. Audre Lorde warned, "The master's tool will never dismantle the master's house" (1984, 112). But is language the master's tool, or does language encompass the master as well? Can we not twist his tools into tinsel? Tools into toys? Tools into tinderboxes?

(I've always hated the metaphor of tools . . . Ludwig may roll over in his grave at this. Tools are forcers. They are required when even brute strength will not get the job done. Tools are instruments of torture—wrenching, pounding, screwing, drilling, chiseling. We do not necessarily want tools.)

Other voices, singing on the sidelines, support us, suggesting scripts for us to follow.

They create the possibility of the woman of means . . . and ways. They can help us to blast out of our prisons—created from low-burning tempers, lolling libidos, lackluster liberalism, loser labels, and ladylikeness.

They give us ruses, diversions, lighthearted banter. We must elude the mainsayers, with no confrontations, no arguments, no logical lies.

It is time for carnival—for glamour, disguise, mystery, and Puckish surprise.

Act III: Acting Out

Can making a spectacle create cultural change?

Through discourses we construct our selves, our desires, our erotic orientations, and our possibilities. How can we create and be created through discourses that brings potential for change?

As Michelle Fine and Susan Gordon suggest, we "need to disrupt prevailing notions of what is inevitable, what is natural, and what is impossible . . . to invent and publish images of what is not now, and what could be" (1991, 24).

We need to draw dirty pictures . . . do unruly things . . . un-ruly . . .
against the rulers, against the rules.

Making it up as we go along.

Woman under construction. Or on Top of??

Topsy-turvy, turning the world upside down . . . or perhaps more
potently, sidling up . . . saddling up.

[Straddling a chair or a stool]

Woman on Top . . . Controlling the pace . . . taking in as much as she
wants. Finding a hipbone for her lipbone.

A missionary in her position, evading the law.

A butterfly wing stroking in sweet rebellion. Stirring up the airwaves
in spunky surrender.

The image of the disorderly woman stirring the cauldron . . . widen
options for women . . . a temporary release, there's no grand solution
anymore.

But Lady Godiva rides, and politics are rampant. *[Perhaps rocking on
the chair or stool throughout this speech]*

So what might we do about the opposite sexes? Can we only count
to two? Or can there be boy-girls and girl-boys, and everything else in
between? Sugary Snakes and spicy snails, and leave the nice puppy dog
tails for the puppies?

Lets make some "gender trouble" as Judith Butler says: myths of gender, however alluring, are the bane of women's lives. Weapon one in our
wayward wars of transgression: fool with Mother Nature; rub on the
line that divides the sexes. (Hmmm that always feels good to rub on that
line.)

Cross over the line, erase the line, blur the line? Is there a politics of
lines? Watch out for the dangerous curves.

*[Perhaps inserting a slightly off-colored joke here: "Have you heard
the one about . . ."]*

But, if gender is performance, there are certain things we've got
to learn. We become the dramatic effect of our performances. We act
out the gestures of gender and age. We are fantasies whose bodies are
inscribed through our performances. We, whoever we are, can affirm
ourselves, while destabilizing the ideal of female beauty and realigning
desire.

Although we are trapped in social orderings, tattooed within our
proper place . . . in outlandish moments we are freed to create the possibility of cultural change . . . Let us go on from here: To revel in our
specialness. To blush only when it suits us. To hold our heads up and be
proud, no matter where and how we are. To celebrate the lifted yoke of
fertility and rejoice in our wholeness again. *[Fanning herself again]* Like
girls, to prance in moonlight and in sun. To remember that the calendar

is only one—bureaucratic—measurement of time. It cannot tell the age of spirit, heart, and mind.

Our spectacles are opportunities to glamour into being other forms of life. As we soar over the edge of respectability (with a bow to Thelma and Louise), let us make a joyful noise and be glad of our excesses. Let us find a way to celebrate. Let us dare to strut our stuff and when we die, die laughing . . .

13

The Costume is the Message

Mary Gergen

The setting for this piece was a symposium on developments in qualitative inquiry at the annual meetings of the American Psychological Association in 2008. At the time I was sensing the many ways in which our culture, and indeed the field of psychology, celebrates separation—mind/body, self/other, person/environment. What was this doing, I wondered, to our being-with the world, or one might say, our creaturely sensual capacities that unite us with nature? Even our scholarly penchant to describe and explain seemed to dull the senses, and in a way, to work against the environmental values that we otherwise extolled. A sensuous performance seemed an answer, one that subverted abstract analysis through concrete action. The costume for the piece played a central role, as I wanted to dress in a way that insulated me from the surrounding world. In what follows I am wearing a silvery floor-length raincoat with a hood that almost covers my face. On my hands are large, plastic oven mitts. I am almost totally covered.

WHAT'S WRONG WITH MY "I"

I feel sometimes that I am shrink-wrapped . . . closed off from the earth . . . I remember that feeling in the mountains where I was walking one summer in a field of wildflowers, somewhere in the Rocky Mountains. I was aware of the undulating grasses, the thousands of wildflowers—pink, blue, purple, golden, and white, the big azure blue sky with fluffy cumulus clouds, the lush clustering evergreen trees on the mountainside, the warm and gentle sun, and the sounds of the natural world surrounding me. Beyond the package of me, there was the unfulfilled promise of the

possibility of an experience of beauty, of rapture, of spiritual fulfillment, powerful and magnificent . . . It was like an inkling of an untold secret, but one that would not be revealed to me. Somehow I didn't know how to slice open the package I was in, the separating spheres of me, even as I lay down in the field to feel it with my body, not just with my eyes. I tried to understand more clearly what I was doing and what I seemed to want. Recalling a literary tradition, I wondered if I was seeking what Thoreau and Emerson described as the transcendental aura, which only exists on the page, and never in the flesh. My shrink-wrapped self is my destiny. Or, I wondered if there could be a way to slip this shell and join in some other way of being in the world.

I think of how we socialize our babies into the world . . . tenderly wrapping them in our Saran-ated way. We learn and teach that who we are is within us, in our private sphere, unreachable, deep within our skulls. Our action center, our sensory center, our self is so impenetrable that we cannot access it, only in our dreams. We learn that a war goes on within, between our feelings and our thoughts, our desires and our principles, and we learn to control the warring factions as best we can. We learn our specialness, our uniqueness, our separateness from all other creatures and things. We take pride in being true to ourselves, independent, free, and self-contained. This separation shrink-wraps us in our places. But often there is a yearning to break through our isolation, to connect again, as we suspect we once could do. How is it possible to break through our individual loneliness . . . that is what we wonder.

[I start taking off my gloves]

There seem to be ways. Let me mention a few:

We meditate, practice Yoga, and sit alone on mats, dreaming with an empty mind, if possible, hoping to escape our separate existences and experience nirvana.

Some choose the route through drugs and alcohol; the sweet elixirs of forgetfulness; others find glimpses of release in sexual encounters, and the ecstasy of love and the grief of death—tragedy and loss . . . For some, only the extremes—jumping out of airplanes, driving racecars, shooting guns, cutting our own flesh . . .

Becoming Mentally Ill frees us, from time to time.

The childlike impulse to play and laugh . . . rolling down the hill . . . digging in the sand, splashing in the mud puddle, licking snowflakes with our tongues, these create momentary ways to lose ourselves in the flow.

Art works: painting, singing, dancing, poetry, drama . . .

All are about losing our specialness . . . our singularity, our egocentrism . . .

Breaking through . . .

What holds us back? Psychology didn't help us . . . Our lessons in individualism . . . our private space . . . our brain-ness . . . our me-ness.

Letting go of my I . . . remaining in connectedness . . . being at one in our relations . . . with nature, animals . . . children, other people . . . notice our skin on the air, in the air, with the air. Our bodies warming the air, the air cooling our bodies . . .

It's time to rethink our positions in space and time. We need a new metaphor . . . a new psychology. What if We are not one, but a wheel of many. We are made from our relationships, past and future, and in-between. If we think of ourselves as socially conceived, as a part of all we touch, as created and cocreating in the moment as we live. If we give up our individuality, and cherish our connections. If we take our relational processes as creating ourselves . . . then what?

Moments and memories of connection . . . all into the oneness of the universe . . . a thrilling encounter . . . endlessly revolving . . . endlessly creating . . . endlessly ending . . . ephemeral . . . untrustworthy . . . momentary . . . resilient . . . careless . . . carefree . . . coming into being through our we-ness.

14

Reflecting on Dramatic Performance

Mary: Why is it that doing performances such as these is so gratifying, satisfying, and edifying? And, why is it that audiences also seem to connect with them in a special way, in a way that a very polished script in the form of a lecture can seldom achieve? Performances give an eyeful as well as an earful. The movement, color, and the drama can envelop the viewer. Emotions and desires are aroused; one can imagine oneself in the drama. And there can also be an eventful quality in a performance, something that is hard to forget. Perhaps you resist what I've said, Ken. That's allowed.

Ken: I surely agree with all this, but yes, I also carry a sack of doubts around with me. You are right, for example, about the power of performance, in contrast to most academic presentations. And you were right to point out that this "can" be the case. But you and I and many people who do this kind of work are amateurs. We don't have the kind of training that can be essential to dramatic work. And one of the essential ingredients of staged drama is that we, as audience, are relaxed enough to get into the content of the work. That is, we are not watching and thinking *about* the actors, but are willing to suspend disbelief. Now, in the case of amateur work, I am not sure the audience can suspend these concerns. Are they watching to see how the performance is going as an academic contribution, whether the performers are at all skilled, and so on? Are they looking at us, as opposed to joining with us?

Mary: You are so right about all of this. If the audience is nervous for the actors, hoping they won't fumble or fall down, or annoyed because they are being subjected to a round of nonsense or an unbearably bad performance, then it is better not to be done. I suspect that doing a performance is challenging enough that only a few brave souls tend to try it. At the same time, if I think of those I have seen, I have not had a bad experience. The levels of performance have been good to great, and certainly more skilled than what one finds in the average lecture given by professional academics. I also think the audience gets revved up in advance when they are going to witness a performance. They are more fully there, in part, because they want to see the fully present performer reveal something personal, in addition to or instead of abstract ideas.

   This mutual coming together creates a bit of magic in the space. On the other hand, what gets me steamed up is when a noted scholar decides that reading the latest chapter from his or her last book is a suitable performance for an eager audience.

Ken: In fact, think about most academic presentations we have heard at conferences . . . where the speaker is either buried in a text and reading in a monotone, or the lights go off and the speaker paraphrases the PowerPoint. Not too thrilling. We have had a long-standing dialogue with the folks at the East Side Institute in New York, as they opt for fully professional performances while we advocate amateurism. Our main concern is that if performative work in the social sciences is reserved for professionals, it will seldom be risked. Further, many academics are quite skilled as amateurs; they have well-developed talents. Others feel the thrill of taking a risk, and feel the urgency of passionate expression. Better a science in which these impulses can flower than one in which we are all forced into the straight jacket of colorless tradition.

Mary: Hurray for that! But you know, one of the things we have also worried about with a lot of our performance work is that it still leaves the audience in the role of spectators. Sure, they are more engaged than they might be with traditional academic writing, but we know from our teaching practices that it would be even better if they were actively engaged in performance. This is one of the reasons I like the Boal tradition in which the spectators are invited into the performance.

Ken: I have just been reading Joe Norris's recent work on playbuilding as qualitative research (2010). Great stuff. He uses what he calls mirror theater to help groups explore issues that matter to them, like prejudice, conflict, sexual relations, risk taking, and so on. Seems to me that work like this also supports the case of amateurism in performance work. If we are not too good at our craft as performers, we invite audiences to try it out for themselves. "I could do that too," they might conclude. One could even argue that the most important outcome of performance work lies in the fact that it encourages others to expand their potentials.

SECTION IV

VISUALIZING IDEAS: BELIEVING IS SEEING

There are many signs that print is slowly giving way to visual communication. Although this seems to be the trend, we scarcely see this as the end of the printed word. It is largely with words that we construct the meaning of events. Many years ago we were rather shocked to find that our young children couldn't care less about sunsets, falling leaves, and mountain ranges; nature in the raw was a bore for them. It was through words that these scenes of nature were later romanticized. And now they marvel at nature's wonders. In the same way, many would fail to appreciate the work of artists such as Picasso, Brancusi, or Dali without verbal commentaries on the history of art. In some cases, a picture requires a thousand words to acquire its worth. However, with the deluge of materials now available on the Internet and other media, an individual's sustained attention is becoming a scarce commodity. We search for increasingly rapid means of absorbing the world's offerings. Alas, reading requires time, and unlike reading, graphic work can often speak with immediacy. The choice between the picture and the thousand words is always with us, and in the contemporary media ecology the picture will tend to win out.

In our own case, there was nothing in our professional education that prepared us for working in visual media. As pastimes we both painted and sketched from time to time, but neither of us was artistically trained. To be sure, we had ample experience with the slim repertoire of visual devices traditionally used by social scientists, i.e. scatter plots, graphs and charts, flow diagrams, and the like. However, not only were these devices constraining, but too often they seemed to interfere with what we wanted to say. In chapter 1 we touched on the way in which visual anthropology and sociology influenced us in early years. At the same time, much of this work seemed based on realist assumptions that the picture was truth bearing. We became more interested in how visuals could be "interpretation bearing." Here we found a great deal of freedom to experiment. How could we expand the scientific playing field in such a way that visual possibilities are unlimited?

In what follows we share a range of excursions into visual expression. Most of this work has been carried out collaboratively with artist friends. And, because of our own text-based training, we have tended to explore visual expression in conjunction with theoretical perspectives. Our hope has frequently been to generate a dialogue between words and visual expression, with the aim of a synergistic outcome. There is an old adage that writing about music is like dancing about architecture. What is conveyed in one medium cannot adequately express what is contained in the other. However, in writing *with* music and dancing *with* architecture, new worlds of possibility are opened.

15

Playing with Sam

Ken Gergen, with Sam Maitin

I am indebted to the Philadelphia artist Sam Maitin for my entry into artistic collaboration. It was one thing to work with Mary in generating the kind of dialogic performances described in the last section, as we had our academic histories to rely on. However, for lack of training, I was more tentative in working with visual materials. In the late 1960s I was fortunate enough to meet Sam at a colloquium I was giving at the University of Pennsylvania's Annenberg School of Communication. It was clear from his remarks that he saw his art as a companion to scholarly ideas. Soon we struck up a conversation, and his mirth, creativity, and warmth led us into a productive friendship. In addition to the "happening" described in chapter 1, we also experimented with combining his artistic work with theoretical ideas I was developing at the time. I had become critical, for example, of the Cartesian idea that reason precedes action. So often, it seemed, my actions were fluidly emerging without any preceding contemplation on my part. For example, here I am typing away at my keyboard and the words just take shape, almost automatically. I am not lost in thought before each word jumps onto the page. It's as if the act of writing now teaches me what I have to say. With such ideas in play, Sam took some words from my writing, and brought forth the following.

See figure 1 in the color insert.

16

Relational Art

Ken Gergen, with Regine Walter

With Sam Maitin's premature death, I felt a diminishment of self. Yet our work together opened me to exploring with other artists. In the mid-1980s I was lecturing at the University of St. Galen, in Switzerland, where a lively friendship with Professor Emil Walter provided just the right opportunity. His wife, Regine Walter, was an emerging figure in the Zurich art world. Her drawings, paintings, and etchings were at the cutting edge of what was taking place. When we were introduced, I found myself struck by the resonance of my writing with many of her drawings and paintings. I asked her if she might work with me in exploring the relationship between her work and my theoretical endeavors at the time. I suggested that as a way of relating to her art, I would attempt to realize some of my theoretical views in a poetic form that would become associated with specific pieces of art. In effect, the poetics and visual might work together. She was open to the challenge, and the result for me was a rich adventure in the visualization of theory and the theorization of the visual.

We called the collaborative outcomes "relational art." Not only were the words and the art related, but they were also both concerned with relationship. I offered a brief introduction to "relational theory" in chapter 8.[1] However, to appreciate what follows it is useful to expand a little further.

Consider the sentence I just wrote. You find words like "however," "appreciate," and "little." Yet, none of these words alone tell us anything. They are just free-floating marks on paper. They only come into meaning when they are placed in a particular relationship with each other. The words require each other to create the meaning you took from that sentence. Now shift the focus from the sentence to our actions together. That is, consider the actions of either of us alone as the equivalent to the individual words in a sentence. Here you rapidly see that neither my action alone—nor yours—would be meaningful in itself. That is, my actions come to be sensible or meaningful only in their relationship to what you do, and vice versa. Thus, for example, my outstretched hand in itself has no particular meaning; it is just a curious event. It begins to acquire its meaning the moment when you begin to shake it. The greeting is not born in my action or your action, but in our coordinated actions (or coaction). And if this is so, then all that we hold meaningful—all that we take to be true, rational, and good—finds its origin not within individual minds but within relational processes.

In the following I include a sample of six relationally oriented works. The first is a critique of the individualist tradition so pervasive in the Western world. The very idea of single, autonomous beings constructs a world of ultimate separation and alienation. It is a world in which we can never truly know or trust each other.

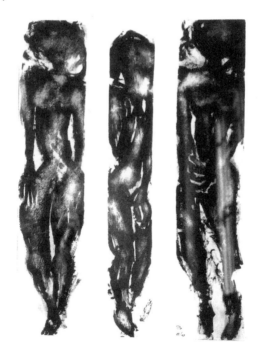

So cozy in here
Just the way I like it
My way, no intrusions.
You may touch, but no entry
No ruffling or mussing about.
It's my life, my future.
Are you listening? Please listen.
Please . . .

In contrast to the individualist tradition, relational theory proposes that we are never truly alone or apart. All that we think and feel, for example, emerges from relationship. From a relational standpoint the visual image of the lone individual is a form of illusion; the boundary of the physical body suggests that one's actions originate within. However, the visual image obscures the relationships of which we are a part, relationships that give the individual the potential to be a "self" whose actions have meaning. The singular image thus functions like the tip of an iceberg in which the larger structure is removed from view. Walter's graphic captures this sensibility for me.

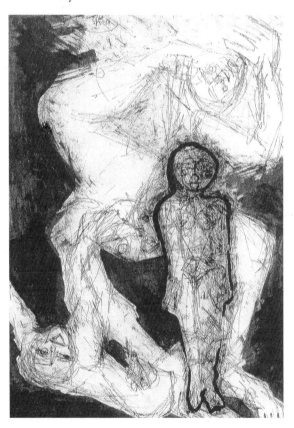

Here I am
Standing before you

Singular and solitary.
But don't let appearances fool you.
Each word from my mouth
Each gesture
Is born of others.

You see singularity
But reality is in multiples.

As we talk
You enter this world
And I into another.

A relational view of the self also calls attention to the significance of tradition or cultural history in giving meaning to contemporary action. If we are cut away from all that precedes us, we have no words and no meaningful actions. In this sense we owe to previous generations the possibility for participating in contemporary life. For me, this next work by Walter evoked these ideas in a powerful way. Out of a dark and swirling vortex of the past come the voices of all those who have gone before us. These voices inhabit our being and express themselves in our ongoing interchange. The dead are never fully lost; our actions ever reveal their presence.

The eternal sounds of the internal voices . . .
Mother . . . father . . . brothers . . . sisters . . .

Listen carefully when I speak
And you shall hear them.

And when they spoke, their words carried echoes
Of mother . . . father . . . brothers . . . sisters . . .

As I speak with you now
You will hear the echoes of distant times.

We typically like to think of our life histories as uniquely ours. However, our very ability to tell a story about ourselves owes a debt to the past. We inherit from the Western tradition various conventions for what constitutes a "good story," conventions that invite us to generate the sense of a "beginning" and an "ending," "high points" and "low points," coherencies and consequents. In this sense, life stories are not records of events as they occurred, but constructions of our lives according to standards of storytelling. This does not make such stories less important; rather, we could not easily participate in contemporary society without them. In the next work, I found in Walter's drawing a storyteller who is portraying a self, but is simultaneously guided by the alter ego of communal tradition.

Here is the story of my life—
Or at least one life
The kind of life
Told by folks like us
The way we tell stories these days.
Some stories are good for laughs
Some stories are tear-jerkers
Where would we be without good stories?
Where would I be without my story?

The next work romanticizes the relational. In the two couplets preceding the final line I tried to show how the joy of relating is created in collaborative action. The pleasure of one cannot be separated from the pleasure of both. In this drawing I was struck by the way in which the two bodies are separate (extensions of other relationships) and yet merged (forming their own relationship out of these extensions).

You are my delight
And your laughter celebrates my being.
My pleasure inhabits your heart,
And my smiles are those of adoration.
Joy resides in the resonance.

In this final work, I again liked the way Regine had generated bodily forms that were simultaneously independent and fused. In the two preceding works I had dwelled on the way in which we bring each other into being. Here, however, I found myself thinking about the ways in which we are also contained through relationship. If we only exist as meaningful persons through others' collaboration, then there is a sense in which others limit what we can be. And yet, the old individualist clamor for freedom and autonomy ("doing it my way") also seems wrongheaded. So, we should see mutual containment not as a negative state, because without it there is simply no meaningful action available to us, no meaning-full future.

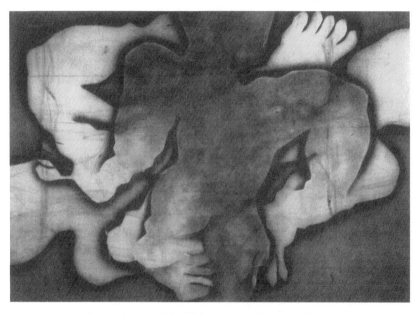

In naming you I build fences round your actions;
Your actions are the fences round my life.
In naming you our future is foreshadowed;
The names we share are the limits of our world.
If we do not name
There is infinite freedom—
But nothing to do.

17

Photographic Playtime

Ken Gergen, with Anne Marie Rijsman-Lecluyse

Photography is such a powerful form of art. A single image, absorbed by the viewer in seconds, can leave an indelible mark. I can sit here, riffing through a pile of photographs, one by one, and they are now part of who I am. How could I find ways of using photography to bring abstract theoretical concepts to life? Could photographs expand on the evocative potentials of theory and compellingly embody the abstract?[1] The photographer Anne Marie Rijsman-Lecluyse (wife of my good friend John Rijsman at Tilburg University) provided the opportunity. Anne Marie was a creative photographer, sometimes adding touches of color to black and white photographs or bringing to life the beauty of otherwise barren landscapes. I approached her about the possibility of working with me in conjoining theory and photography. She was curious, and with this a richly rewarding relationship was born.

In the following I wish to share a range of works that should more properly be called *visual plays*. They represent momentary inspirations, followed by conversations with Anne Marie on the potentials, then moving to ongoing exchanges in which we mutually shaped a visual idea. Her aesthetic sensibility and fine craftwork accounted for the rest.

Most of these collaborations extended the relational theme threading its way through the preceding sections. An early challenge was to use photography to break the illusory spell of individual or independent actors—me here and you there. When we watch people relating, our gaze usually focuses on the individual actors. But this blinds us to the simultaneity of action, what I earlier called coaction, from which meaning derives. Here we try to shift the viewer's gaze to the "space between," using connective words to fill what might otherwise seem like vacant space between two bodies.

In later theorizing I began to think about the limits of focusing on the relationship among human actors alone. After all, our ability as human beings to make sense together ultimately depends on our environmental surrounds. Or, to extend Heidegger's terms, we should think in terms of a relational *being-in-the-world* (Heidegger 1962). For me this idea of uniting persons and environment in collaborative action was later articulated in terms of *confluence*.[2] Human intelligibility rests on the momentary "flowing together" of all. Anne Marie served up just the right illustration for the concept. Remove the bubbles and what sense is there in the coactive movements of mother/daughter?

Relational theorizing was also beginning to take another turn for me. Where much of my early thinking had been centered on ongoing processes—realities in the making—I began to focus increasingly on what people bring into relationships. Clearly we bring to the meaning-making process our linguistic skills, but this seems minimal. I bring not only linguistic skills, but also entire repertoires of action—the movements of my limbs, the direction of my gaze, the tone of my voice, and so on. More importantly, all these skills were born within relationships. Effectively, I bring with me into any relationship a large range of resources drawn from other relationships. And these relationships extend back in time to childhood. For example, I carry with me the capacity to imitate my father, mother, brothers, and so on. And I carry the ways I came to behave in relationship to them. Now, extend this history to include the enormous array of relationships in which we participate over the life course, and you quickly realize that our relational resources are enormous. Working with Anne Marie, we emerged with the following visualization of this *multi-being*.[3] In terms of the self, "I am the common intersection of multiple relationships."

See figure 2 in the color insert.

Yet, this visualization of the person was insufficient. While it reflects the repertoire we bring into relationships, it fails to account for the way in which these resources are mobilized (or not) in the moment at hand. What is brought to life, and what is suppressed? This depends on collaborative action with another multi-being, with whom we sustain and create worlds of meaning. An audience in Greece helped me to see these two adjoining figures as wings of a butterfly (see image below). It is only when both wings move together that the butterfly is lofted into the air.

Other audiences raised the sticky question of authenticity. If we understand the person as constituted within a history of relationships, what are we to make of the common distinction between authentic and inauthentic behavior? Certainly the distinction is important in daily life. We want people to be authentic in their relations with us. Our trust depends on it. But if all our actions are effectively borrowed from the past, in what sense are they authentic? If you declare your love for someone, you will invariably rely on a tradition of words and actions to express yourself. You cannot declare your love by lying face down on the floor. You would certainly be original, but your action would be nonsense. Or, more provocatively, to be an authentic self, is not to be yourself. For the present experiment, authenticity was translated as "serious," and the

See figure 3 in the color insert.

inauthentic as "play." How are we to distinguish the difference? Not, it seems, in our view of the act in itself. To stimulate discussion on this issue, we coaxed Anne Marie's son Thomas into "doing anger." Now we may ask, was he sincere?

18

Visual Deconstruction

Ken Gergen, with Anne Marie Rijsman-Lecluyse

As our photo play continued, so did the experiments in visualizing ideas. I began to think, in particular, of ways of realizing some of the implications of the constructionist ideas that had opened the performative path for us in the first place (see chapter 1). For constructionists, the word "truth" can be dangerous. It can suggest that a particular way of putting things is superior to all others. If we possess "the truth" there is no need for further discussion. All contrary voices are silenced. How could we use visual means of undermining transcendent declarations of truth? Here we focused on one of the weak points in traditional views of truth, namely its dependency on a picture theory of language. In this tradition, theoretical language should be driven by what there is in the world. Figuratively, if we spy a cat and a dog and a mouse in the room, then we should require these three words (or their equivalent) to describe the existing condition. And when this description is shared with others, they could enter the room and evaluate whether this was so. In effect, the words would be an accurate picture of what is the case. However, such an account requires that the relationship between word and referent remain stable. The account would only be true if all parties used words in the same way at all times. Here was an opening to the visual: could we demonstrate that the use of words is always context specific, dependent on how we use them in a particular time and place? This would help us realize that meaning is always in motion. Declarations of Truth are suppressive: they arrest motion.

In this photographic triad we attempt to restore movement. In the first effort, we try to show that the common words "inside" and "outside" carry no definitive meaning. Whatever is "outside" is always an "inside" and vice versa. In the second, we attempt to deconstruct the common distinction between figure and ground. As illustrated, there is no way of declaring the nature of figure and ground, as every figure can also be ground. In the final work, we take an array of words that designate place—up vs. down, East vs. West, and so on. Through visual rearrangement, the word meaning is undermined. Up is also down, East is also West . . .

Inside/Outside

Figure/Ground

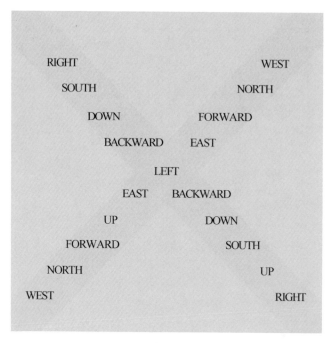

Left/Right

19

Reflecting on Visual Performance

Mary: Surveying these adventures, I am struck first of all by the long and creative career you have had over the years as a visual artist in partnership with our colleagues and friends. My definition of you has really been enlarged by this work that has seeped into our lives over the decades. Your escapades with sketches, paints, and photos have become invested with special significance. I am also impressed with the integration of your theoretical ideas, especially about relational theory, into the artistic work. Bringing together visual symbols with abstract ideas is liberating, not only to those who are involved in the arts, but also to those who are more verbally oriented.

More generally, it seems to me that what you are doing illustrates how academic text can really be enriched through visual media. The visual enriches the verbal. But I also have reservations about this idea. I wonder in particular if the visual is, in some fashion, already verbalized. Do visual productions implicitly contain verbal codes that give them meaning? An experiment I did with photography in 1988 emphasizes the point that visual images without implicit codes are largely meaningless (Gergen and Gergen 1991). In this case, photographs were not worth a thousand words as the saying goes, but rather, without the one thousand words, they were worth very little. In my little experiment, I took a photograph straight ahead of me every twenty minutes for twelve hours. (It was quite a fascinating day that included a stroll in a Malaysian mountain, and flying to Singapore.) After the photos were developed I laid them out in timely order, and I asked various people to tell me a story about them: "What was happening?" Adults had almost no ability to make sense of the array. Only a small boy could pick out items at random and give an answer ("That is an airport ticket counter"). He was too young to try to invent a reasonable story, and the disjunctions did not faze him. One of my intuitions from this experiment was that pictures make sense to us because they are already encoded and have a limited potential of possible meanings. Wedding photographs, for example, must be of a certain form to convey a sense of the occasion. A photo of the shoes of the bride and the bride's father as he walks her down the aisle would not pass muster in a wedding album; a photo of the bridal bouquet would. In many of your examples in this section there is a marriage of pictorial elements and words. However, the pictorial already has to carry a meaning related to the visual in order to make the blending work.

Ken: I like your point very much, and clearly the capacity of an image to enrich and expand on the accompanying words depends in large measure on the history of the image in the meaning-making process. However, I wonder how we might best understand the "meaning of the image." You mention at one point that it is in a sense "verbalized," but then go on to show, at least as I see it, that the photos of a wedding only have meaning if they are related to a history of wedding photos. In this case, the verbalization doesn't seem too important. It's a visual history that counts. So, we could have word meaning in itself (as in a word game), and picture meaning in itself (as in a visual retrospective of an artist); and we could have overlaps (visuals connected to word games, and the retrospective accompanied by remarks from an art critic). But this does set the stage, it seems to me, for a lot of catalytic creativity. Poets open new vistas of understanding with surprising juxtapositions of words, in the same way as artists can unsettle our visual habits with unusual combinations of color, form, or content. We are not, then, victims of preexisting codes. And in the case of word/image combinations, the possibility for new meaning potentials, born within unsettling juxtapositions, seems enormous.

Let me ask you in this context—speaking to you as a social scientist—did you find some of the experiments above more successful than others, and can you tell me why?

Mary: Interesting point you make, as well! But the question of "success" in combining words and image is complicated; there are so many criteria we might use. For example, we might ask, which of the experiments is the most code-dependent? Which of them would be best grounded in the cultural vernacular? You could look at cultural grounding as an indicator of success; the audience could grasp what you are saying. The combination would have more power than if you used words and image independently. Yet, the downside of familiarity is banality. For example, the word "love" and a picture of a red heart are so entangled that nothing new can be imagined from that valentine. If one juxtaposes a less familiar image with a word, the effect might be more powerful, as long as the connection were made. Let's suggest that "love" and an image of a "thunderstorm" might be quite a provocative combination, which could lead to more novel thoughts about love (and thunderstorms).

Another standard for judging the success of a combination would have to do with complexity. Thinking of the pieces in this section, I wonder if the more complex the concept is, the simpler or more explicit the image needs to be. And perhaps vice versa. For me, the most successful examples in chapter 17 are the one- and two-winged "butterfly" images. We have used them very often in lectures and workshops to illustrate the idea of the relational self. I like the way they enrich the idea of the complexity and potentials of two people coming together, and negotiating what selves they will become as they engage in a relational process. The relational approach is difficult for novices to fully grasp, as it flies in the face of conventional wisdom, so the images of the butterfly have been very helpful in introducing novelty.

Another way of assessing the effectiveness of the experiments in this section might be to rate the harmony of the word/image combinations. The first illustration, the piece with Sam Maitin, seems wonderfully harmonious. The words are indeed part of the image. On the other hand, the drawings of Regine Walter are extremely complex, and to my taste, not the best match for your poetic renditions, which are unique in linguistic style, but rather direct in their message. Your work with Anne Marie Rijsman-Lecluyse varies a lot in this respect. Sometimes you both use very direct or pointed combinations, but with others your message seems a bit too ambiguous a match for the photo productions.

I suspect that for many people, aesthetic criteria would be primary. Are the words, the images, and the ways in which they are assembled beautiful or fascinating or otherwise attracting? This question is beyond the scope of the social science perspective, but extremely important from a performative point of view.

Ken: So, I guess we can scrap the idea of a report card. So many criteria, and none of them with clear foundations. This also means that different audiences will have different kinds of reactions, and that the reactions to a given work will change across time. I do think it's important to keep these kinds of critical standards in mind in doing performative work. And it would be interesting to expand on what sorts of criteria people will bring to bear. But in the end, I guess you just put your work out there, and hope that someone, somewhere, can find nourishment. We approach our audiences like trapeze artists—flying through the air, suspended over a pit of meaninglessness—hoping that someone will grasp our efforts and help them fly into the stratosphere.

SECTION V

EXTENDING EXPERIMENTS: FLYING FURNITURE

When you open the door to the performative, be prepared: all the furniture begins to fly. You enter perhaps tentatively, conservatively, cautiously, and with few models from which to draw. You may simply add a new twist to your writing, a new voice, a flirtation with a new genre. Or perhaps you embellish the writing with an illustrative photograph or cartoon. The excitement begins. Soon enough, you begin to see that writing has its limits, and you begin to peer over the fence at other forms of expression. Now immersed—or you might say "bitten"—you begin to see the world anew. Where there was once a "tradition to follow," there is now a profusion of invitations to experiment. Hmmm . . . why not try adding this, mixing that . . .? The question of "why not try . . ." increasingly pervades and persuades, and this voice is intensified by the flowing of the creative juices. Excitement then gives way to a giddy feeling of vertigo. Nothing remains stable, no tradition is beyond question, and what had been your "work" gives way to passionate and purposeful play.

In this final section of the book we share the results of our own playroom adventures. These are instances in which we have moved beyond traditional genres of literature, drama, and the visual arts, as treated in previous sections. In most cases these are, in Geertz's terms (1983), *blurred genres*. In almost all these cases we have experienced a certain degree of fear, moving beyond borders of familiarity. As Mary Douglas (1966) might say, when we exit the domain of the pure, we enter territories of danger. Yet, the spirited excitement of working in these unfamiliar zones eclipsed our fear. And, suspecting that our audience for such efforts might also be suffering from self-doubts, we could hope for some sympathy for our failings. So that others may be encouraged to carry forward their projects in more daring and effective ways, we share explorations into social science as sculpture, cartooning, music, multimedia, cyberpolitics, word-forms, haiku, and pedagogical practice.

20

Sculpting Ideas

Ken Gergen

In earlier years I fancied the possibility of taking up sculpting as a pastime. However, after spending some illuminating hours with a professional sculptor, it became clear to me that this fantasy would remain dormant. As I marveled at the large stone that was, through his efforts, becoming an object of great beauty, I also realized that he had been chipping away for almost a year on the project. This was no "pastime"; it was full time. However, the growing use of found objects in the sculpting community seemed to open brightening possibilities. The special challenge for me, then, was to think of ways I could link such activity to my scholarly interests. I wasn't interested in traditional, representational sculpture, nor did the modernist view of sculpture as non-referential—form for the sake of form—appeal to me. Would it be possible to bring abstract ideas into physical form, in much the same way that drama and art had been used in the preceding work?

My earliest move in this direction actually took place in the late 1970s. The sculpted properties of a piece of Styrofoam caught my eye. As an abstraction, one could imagine a human being, and the indention in the "head" could be viewed as an eye. I was already reading theorists concerned with relational process, and then it struck me! Charles Horton Cooley had written in 1902 about self-understanding as a reflection of other people's perception:

Each to each a looking-glass
Reflects the other that doth pass.

Or, in Cooley's compelling metaphor, we are "looking-glass selves." With the help of a mirror, paint, and gypsum, the result was what I called *The Looking-Glass Self*: an object that brings the viewer into being through mirrored reflection (see figure next page).

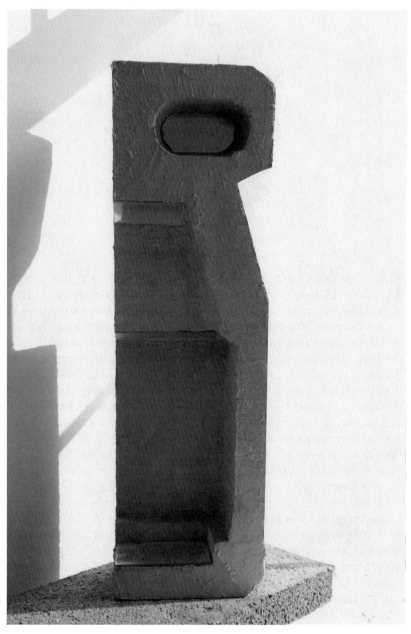

Looking-Glass Self

A second and more recent exploration was stimulated by the fact that winters in Pennsylvania can bring about long periods of cold, grey weather, accompanied by a monochromatic wilderness. Sometimes when I looked from the window, I had the feeling of being imprisoned by nature. Nothing bright, vivid, or enlivening in sight. Why not, then, insert color into nature? And better still, what if this way of supplementing nature could reflect the kinds of relational ideas discussed in the preceding chapters? With four 4×4's, preservatives, paints, brushes, concrete, and the help of friends, the idea came to life: an abstract expression of a family unit, with each of the four members carrying a distinctive color, along with the colors of each of the others. In effect, each member of the family is unique, but also fundamentally symbiotic. I call the piece *Fantasy Family*, not only because it suggests some idealized family of two genders and two children, all nicely bonded, but also because this blaze of color in the midst of a grey winter is nothing but fantasy.

A final adventure into the plastic arts is more radical. One thing that had bothered me about the Fantasy Family was that it seemed an intrusion into nature. It might suggest an insufficiency in nature, for which I, as an alien superior, was attempting to provide the antidote. How,

Fantasy Family
See figure 4 in the color insert.

I asked, could one work with nature so that the idea of fundamental relatedness could find significant expression?

Working with nature in this instance had special significance. Relational theory has been primarily concerned with relationships among human beings, and as Slife and Richardson (2011) properly pointed out, this is a limited vision. My book, *Relational Being* (2009b), had attempted to bring physical objects into the confluence of meaning-making, and had touched on the possibility of linking relational theory with environmentalism, but I needed to move further. Here I began to think of recent trends in biology that challenged the traditional Darwinian view of the survival of the fittest. In particular, many biologists are moving toward theories of *coevolution*, where survival depends on collaboration among species, as opposed to competition. I also thought of recent research on the way our bodily health depends on some ninety trillion microbes we carry inside us. Yet, at the same time, we also tend to perceive nature in terms of independent entities—trees, flowers, bushes, and so on. Would it be possible, I asked, to somehow bend perception so that the interdependence in nature would be brought into visual reality? Then it occurred to me that in a nearby forest there were hundreds of maple seedlings growing. Each seedling could be seen as separate, but in fact they shared a common origin. To emphasize this origin, I knotted branches of the seedlings together to form a canopy of connection. I call this a *Symbiotic Sanctuary*, and the remnants can be found even after two years.

Symbiotic Sanctuary
Photo courtesy of Anne Marie Rijsman-Lecluyse

21

Cartooning and Critique

Mary Gergen

Both my feminist and constructionist leanings have fostered a critical view of the empiricist tradition in the social sciences. So often, it seems, empiricist methods function as impersonal, mechanical devices that force people into categories largely irrelevant to life as they understand and live it. But how can critiques of these methodologies be communicated in such a way that even those who are "vicitimized" by them can understand? And how can they be carried out in such a way that the critic doesn't claim some kind of moral superiority? One answer is to explore the age-old practice of cartooning. Critique with a light touch. So, I tried my hand at several critical cartoons. One thing I especially liked about them was their capacity to communicate in a flash the essentials of an argument that might take pages to unfold. And they might simultaneously evoke a giggle and a nod. Our son-in-law, Lee Bell, contributed to the images with his skillful renditions of my humble characters.

Actually, Mrs. Jones, I don't want to know what you REALLY think. Just answer the question, please.

Well, it must mean something, Harry!!

Now you are to carry on a normal conversation about any topic you wish. Don't let us disturb you.

22

To Song!

A dding musical performance to scientific work always seemed a stretch. Our musical training was limited, and to link music to scholarship was a real challenge. How could music be used to express complex theoretical ideas? Yet, there were possibilities—on the light side, Tom Lehrer's musical send-ups, and on the heavy, Richard Strauss' rendition of Nietzchian philosophy in *Also Sprach Zarathustra*. So, we ultimately gave ourselves permission to play. In the earliest instance, one of us (Ken) was invited to give an autobiographical presentation to a therapy conference. Who was the person behind the ideas, and how was his personal life related to his work? Such a request suggested a lighter touch, one more akin to song. The result was a musical prelude to the verbal account, one in which Ken did an a cappella collage of songs— including pop, country and western, pep rally songs, rock, and the like— to represent the changes he went through in his earlier years. One result of this experience was that Mary decided to purchase a five-string banjo as a gift for her mate, knowing that in his graduate student days he had participated in folk music get-togethers. This led, in turn, to the two of us occasionally singing banjo-accompanied duets at birthdays and wedding dinners. We were coming to understand that the music could really intensify the content of what we were trying to communicate, much the same way that the musical background in movies transforms the scenes.

An opportunity to apply this understanding soon arrived. We were invited to present a plenary address at an international conference on critical psychology in Bath, England. Although we had done a good deal of critical work, some of which is represented in this volume, we had also developed doubts about it. Critique typically invites countercritique, and then mutually frozen animosities. These animosities are further fueled by the moral high ground claimed by both parties. In effect, we felt the critical movement in psychology was producing less in the way of change than permanent polarization.

At the conference there were multiple factions—Marxists, constructionists, critical realists, feminists, gay and lesbians, anticolonialists, and so on. These small groups not only shared in their critiques of mainstream psychology, but had also begun to express antipathy for each other. Marxists didn't approve of constructionists, feminists felt left out of the Marxist agenda, and so on. Presenters at such conferences were often subjected to audience assassinations. In our presentation we wanted to criticize all of this, essentially subjecting our colleagues to a critique of critique. Yet, how could we engage in critique without using the very form of expression we were placing in question? Our answer was song. Why not compose a humorous song poking fun at critique—our own included? The result was a duet, accompanied by banjo:

Stirring The Bath Water
(to the tune of "Keep on the Sunny Side")

Keep on the critic's side, always on the critic's side
Keep on the critic's side of life
It will help us every day, all the evil we will slay,
If we keep on the critic's side of life.

Behaviorism is now down the drain,
Cognition is also found lame,
Psychoanalysis is universalist,
And evolution simply up the twist.

Keep on the critic's side, always on the critic's side
Keep on the critic's side of life
It will help us every day, moral high ground is our way
If we keep on the critic's side of life.

If you don't treat matters material
You'll be damned for being ethereal,
But if you put material on your list
You are a dirty essentialist

Keep on the critic's side, always on the critic's side
Keep on the critic's side of life
It will help us every day, it will let us march in May,
If we keep on the critic's side of life.

If human desire is your game
Individualism is your rotten name,
And if a constructionist you be
On your relativism we shall pee.

Keep on the critic's side, always on the critic's side
Keep on the critic's side of life
It will help us every day, put the mainstream in dismay,
If we keep on the critic's side of life.

When you march to realism's drums,
Constructionists will get you with their guns,
And if you speak of private experience,
The Pomos will find you very dense.

Keep on the critic's side, always on the critic's side
Keep on the critic's side of life
It will help us every day, it may even boost our pay,
If we keep on the critic's side of life.

If you don't mention gender, race, and class,
You will soon be kicked in the ass,
If you do praise the noble poor
For your exoticizing you'll be shown the door

Keep on the critic's side, always on the critic's side
Keep on the critic's side of life
It will help us every day, with such certainty we can slay,
If we keep on the critic's side of life.

In the future we've done each other in
No one left with analytic sin
What is there now for us to do
Face the world . . . alas . . . still in a stew.

[last stanza, slowly]
If we keep on the critic's side, always on the critic's side
If we keep on the critic's side of life
We kill us every day, is there not another way
Than remaining on the critic's side of life?

23

The Power of Multimedia

Ken Gergen

If the addition of music to words can bring us into new spaces of communication, why not expand the modalities? Why not, for example, add music and visuals to words? And what if the visuals also combined dance and drama? So many possibilities, so little time. In my earliest escapades I enlisted the help of Yongsoo Park, a talented and blithely creative student at Swarthmore College. We began splicing together video and film clips from pop culture for purposes of social commentary. Perhaps the most ambitious was a short film, *Telos in Wonderland*, concerned with identity in postmodern cultural conditions. Here we used small clips from the movies and television, each clip embarking on a narrative that was interrupted by yet another narrative—life as a discontinuous set of events, often juxtaposed in ludicrous ways. We also included a clip revealing us in dialogue about whether to include ourselves in the work. Our lives too were present, and then absent.

In later work I tried to turn the relational artwork discussed in chapter 16 into theater performances. On these occasions the lights were dimmed and I read the poetic fragments as the images were displayed on a large screen. To the combination of sound and image I added mood with the ethereal music of Charlie Hayden's *Magico*. To me in any case the effect was striking. In another instance, Mary and I had presented a number of the relational vignettes described in chapter 10 at a 1995 conference in Huddersfield, England. We felt something was needed, however, to bring the presentation to a concluding climax. By chance we had come across a description of J.S. Bach as he led a choral performance in Leipzig in the early 1700s. By this account, Bach's engagement in the music was total. Not only were his arms waving as he directed the chorus and orchestra, but his body swayed to the rhythms as he literally danced to the music. He and the music and the chorus were one . . . a relational sublime! So, to conclude the presentation, we invited the audience into what we called a relational *imaginary*: fantasizing themselves at the Leipzig Thomaskirche, perhaps as part of the chorus, the orchestra, or as Bach himself. Then, with the sounds of his *Christmas Oratorio* playing in the background, the description of Bach's engagement was read. And as the words trailed to a close, the volume was increased until the sounds of music filled the room. With the magnificent ending of the piece, there was silence . . . and we left the stage.

Perhaps my most complete multimedia presentation was in response to an invitation to present at a 1998 Fordham conference honoring the legacy of Marshall McLuhan. Given McLuhan's famous phrase "the medium is the message," I felt there was no way I could simply present an academic paper. Somehow, the media had to be enlisted in the effort. My book *The Saturated Self*, published some years earlier (1991), had focused on the way in which technologies of communication were radically expanding the number and range of other people in our lives. I had been optimistic about the possibility of global connectivity and integration. However, it had also struck me that these same technologies brought groups together in ways that insulated or alienated them from others. For example, the World Wide Web—with all its individually separated websites—approximated an archipelago of isolated enclaves, each seeking to strengthen and expand its influence. I thus began to assemble a set of slides, each taken from a website that proclaimed the truth and right of its position (e.g. the KKK, white supremacy groups, ultraconservative religious groups). At the same time, Sean Peterson, another bright and unusually gifted student in my Swarthmore course on technology, had constructed for his class project an audiotape composed of sound bites from the "culture of aggression" or, essentially, American culture in the age of technology. One bite was taken from a radio preacher lambasting "godless homosexuals," and the other was a phrase from Clint Eastwood's *Dirty Harry*, "Shoot'm in the m . . . f . . . head." Both were simultaneously righteous and evil. One bite followed the other in succession, and as the tape progressed the sound bites were sped up. As the space between them receded they morphed into an indecipherable wail. This was just the technology I needed. After a verbal introduction, the room was darkened and the slides began to march across the screen to the accompaniment of the audiotape. As the wailing of those hate-filled voices increased, both the amplification and the rapidity with which the slides moved across the screen were increased. At a point of peak intensity, both sound and slides were terminated. The room remained dark and silent. The presentation was complete.

24

Cybergraphics

Ken Gergen, with Anne Marie Rijsman-Lecluyse

A major problem with much performance work is its ephemeral character. Unlike publications or film, the performance is there and gone, with no obvious traces. The passionate performance of a political view may set the heart in motion, but who knows whether it is ever cashed out in terms of social change. Does anything follow? In this context I was reminded of the work of a writer who had emailed a partially completed story to another writer friend, asking him to add to the story and then send it on to another writer. Presumably the work would continue to build and circulate without principled end—a never-ending trace. How, I asked, could such a process be incorporated into performative social science? Could there be ways of inserting performative work into cybernetworks, such that it could be continuously shared? Could it enjoy—at least in principle—a life without end?

While thinking about these possibilities, I also happened to be occupied with what I viewed as the pharmaceutical drugging of the country. The alliance between the profession of psychiatry, the pharmaceutical industry, and the insurance companies generated a means of declaring an increasing proportion of the population as "ill" and in need of medication, for which the insurance companies (drawing income from the population) would pay. For example, within a span of several decades, antidepressant drugs had grown from a multimillion to a multibillion dollar business, and a tenth of the population was destined to be taking them. It was also ironic that at the same time a major "war on drugs" was taking place on the national level. So, we had a situation in which being "high and happy" was policed in such a way that corporate profits were ensured. The situation remains today!

Putting these joint concerns together, I developed a series of "cybergraphics," photographic pieces that could be distributed via email to friends, who in turn could share them with others, and so on. Again drawing from the artistic skills of Anne Marie Rijsman-Lecluyse, we emerged with the pieces below.

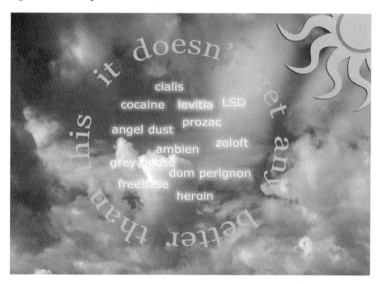

See figure 5 in the color insert.

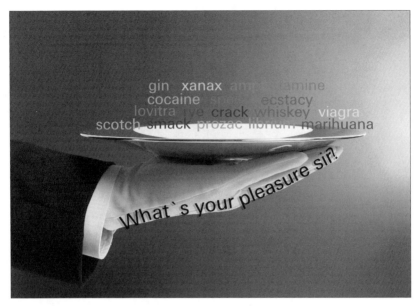

See figure 6 in the color insert.

25

Fragmented Moments: Haiku

Mary Gergen

In the world of literature, the poem is the ultimate form of condensed meaning-making. During our stay in Japan I had also come to love the way in which Japanese haiku poems could illuminate moments in time, at once freezing them and deepening our understanding and appreciation. Further, in the space of seventeen syllables, this momentary glimpse could also carry profundity. For example, an ancient haiku by Basho:

> In the cicada's cry
> No sign can foretell
> How soon it must die.

I also liked the way the haiku challenged the more Cartesian orientation to order and organization. Rather than trying to place all one's observations and insights into an overarching theory, the haiku invited a many-faceted multiplicity. With these views at hand, I began to use haiku as a means of "describing" events. First, I share a recounting of a fiftieth class reunion, filled with various moments of remembrance and contemplation. This is followed by a haiku account of a social constructionist conference in Cancun, Mexico.

A CLASS REUNION: IN HONOR OF THE 50TH CLASS REUNION AT ST. LOUIS PARK HIGH SCHOOL, CLASS OF 1956

> Joy to reunite!
> Perhaps if we are lucky
> We find a lost self.

Years collapse into a pile
Making a confusing, rubbled
Treasure trove.

Neural pathways slashed open
As memories return.
I cannot sleep.

Hard to believe, but here
I make a new friend
From an old acquaintance.

Lined faces and old eyes
Glide into youth
As dusk darkens into night.

Looking into eyes
across the years
We find our young togetherness.

Grey coals of passion, long asleep,
Spark in the breath
Of a gentle fanning.

We cry as we embrace.
Do our hearts know it may be
For the last time?

For tonight the clock plays the fool.
Is Death no wiser for the disguise?

IN HONOR OF THE CONFERENCE "COLLABORATIVE AND DIALOGIC PRACTICES FOR THERAPY AND SOCIAL CHANGE," APRIL 24, 2010, CANCUN, MEXICO

Blue ocean softly sways.
A tempting, but distant dream for us ashore.

Glittering translucent fishes of words
Spring to life as they twirl.

Resounding, Re-sounding
Spanish, English
We hear with two ears or four?

The "C's" of our philosophy:
Critical, creative, constructing.

Bring forthing the "D's" of
dialogue, drama, dance, and dedication.

Rhizomatic structures run deep,
appear in mad proliferation.

Why not say yes,
    say maybe
    say we might?
We could explore together.

Those who have died still live in us.
We cherish their words, as we transgress.

We part, in laughter and in tears,
dancing in the sands
before the sea.

26

Teaching through Fiction

Mary Gergen

We have not commented on the use of performative approaches to teaching. This could be the subject for an entirely new book, as a movement toward performance pedagogy is emerging across the disciplines.[1] The inspirations are many, including the early work of Freire (1970) and Boal (1979), along with Foucault's metaphor of the "docile body" (1975), which reminds us that resistance to oppression must be embodied. Multiple works on the performed character of gender, homosexuality, race, and disability have also encouraged teaching as performance as a means for social change. The two of us have been drawn to the possibilities of performative pedagogy for many years. While our concerns have been partly political, we have also found that in contrast to monological lecturing, students become enthusiastically engaged in relevant performance work. We have often used various forms of role-play and autobiographical writing to these ends. Ken has also asked students in some of his advanced classes to abandon the traditional term paper, and to generate a "term performance" in whatever form they wished. I attended one of the evenings at the end of semester when the students presented their work for each other. There were plays, poetry, painting, photography, dance, multimedia, video, hip-hop . . . on and on. And the students heaped appreciation on each other. The excitement and enthusiasm were unforgettable. Thus, as a way of tipping our hats to performative practices in education, we include this final story.

In 2008 we joined communication scholar Stuart Schrader in publishing a reader in interpersonal communication. One of the readings we hoped to include was an excerpt from a conversation between Queen Latifah and a group of adolescents. We wanted to use the reading to generate discussion on the body as communication, and the problems of being overweight. At the last minute, however, we failed to get permission to use the piece. Thus, I decided it might be interesting to write a fictional dialogue to replace Latifah. I realized in writing the piece that I could actually generate materials more specifically relevant to the issues I thought important. This triggered a fantasy of how one could rewrite textbooks . . . again the furniture began to stir.

YOUR BODY AS COMMUNICATION

We define ourselves for others not only in our talk and dress, but also in how we talk about the shape of our bodies. In the same way that different groups construct different realities and moralities, so do they generate different conceptions of "the good body." This is most obvious in the case of the communities of ballet dancers and body builders. Here we find dramatic differences in what counts as a "good body." Teenage circles also establish standards for what is acceptable in their community. In the following reading we offer a fictionalized account of a group of five teenage girls[2] who meet after school to enjoy each other's company, watch the "soaps" and, in the mix of conversation, end up talking about their bodies.

Patty: What's going on here? I had a Diet Coke in the fridge, and somebody took it. I know it wasn't you, Gail-the-Rail because you just finished off the ice cream. Hey, who's on a diet here anyway . . . or rather who isn't?

Charlene: Don't be so dramatic, Patty, I drank it, and you know there's another case in the fridge downstairs. Anyway, where's the remote so I can get the tv on? And meanwhile, why doesn't somebody go down and bring up some more Diet Coke.

Sally: Hey, not me. I don't even like diet drinks, even if I am always on a diet. I just hate my thighs . . . all that ugly cellulite.

Gail: I wish I had some cellulite. I don't have any curves. I need something more up here and a rounder butt. How am I supposed to be a cheerleader with this body? And look at my arms; they are like rails.

Patty: No kidding, Gail! That's why I call you "Gail-the-Rail."

Charlene: But, Gail's the only one skinny enough to be a model.

Kathy: Maybe, but she's not tall enough. You know this is a crazy group, height-wise. Half of you are short, and the rest of you are tall. Almost no one is my height. You'd think I'd feel normal around you all, but I feel out of it. Either I'm looking up or down all the time.

Sally: Big deal! I wish I were five inches shorter. The only guys I can date are basketball players. Everyone else thinks I'm a giraffe. I always have to wear flats. I hate how tall I am! And it's not fair! Patty's barely five feet and her lover boy, McGoo, is almost twice as tall as she is. Why can't the short girls leave the tall guys for us?

Charlene: I kind of like being short. I can go out with any a guy—short or tall. Trouble is, they're just all so stupid! I can't wait'til I can meet some guys at college, who might at least say something interesting. The guys in our class are so immature.

Gail: I'd just be happy to go out with a guy who was my height or even shorter—especially if he's a jock.

Patty: If I were in the shower, and suddenly somebody pulled away the curtain, you know what I'd cover up? My forehead. I hate my forehead. That's the worst part about my body. That's why I always wear bangs. My mom agrees with me, probably because she also has the same ugly forehead.

Kathy: That's crazy. How can anybody not like their forehead? Besides, you have great lips, and a terrific boyfriend. For me it's clear, I'd cover up my hips. Today, Jon called me "Hippo-hips" again. I hate that, and besides, I don't even think I have big hips. Do I? Certainly not like some other people I could mention who aren't currently among us—like Cherry!

Sally: Yeah, but Cherry has such big breasts, no one even notices if she's got big hips. And you know, what I really can't stand is the way she walks. Like, the girl waddles. She is sooo weird.

Charlene: I hear she took ballet classes . . . That's why they all walk like ducks. I think all Buzzy ever really sees are those 38D's. It makes me want to vomit.

Kathy: I don't know about Buzzy, but I think Jon likes me because he's always making fun of me so that he can get me to look at him.

Sally: In your dreams, girlfriend. Barb's got him under her thumb, even if he does lust after your bod.

Kathy: Why can't you agree with me just once? You'd better be nice or you'll be walking home.

Charlene: Girls, girls, who cares about what the guys think or don't think. There's never been another group like ours to hit this school. Mr. Alwin even told me that we are the cutest and coolest group that he's ever taught. You can tell by the way the other girls look at us that they agree with him. We are sharp!

Patty: Yeah, lets drink to that! Now somebody go get me that Diet Coke. I'm dying.

27

Reflecting on Extended Experiments

Ken: One thing that struck me about so many of our adventures is the way they were "context driven." We didn't often generate a project spontaneously, out of the blue. Often, it seems, we were responding to a specific invitation—to present at a conference, for example, or contribute a chapter or an article. For me this has really been helpful because it has allowed me to imagine a specific audience, interested in a particular set of issues. So, I am motivated not only to create something, but also to communicate or be with others in a way that will engage them. I would like to say "delight," "inform," and "entertain," but I also know there will be many who are alienated or even offended. In any case, there is a lot of motivated joy in thinking about audience appreciation.

Mary: I don't disagree with you, but for me, I think the need to create is powerful, and the need to disseminate is secondary. Many of my entries in this book have been semiprivate for example the haiku on my class reunion. I simply feel, in a given moment, like trying something out. Perhaps later I think about showing it to others. My old English teacher, Mr. Jack Alwin, later contacted me to ask if he could read my haiku in a speech he was giving to another reunion class. That was a thrill! I also wonder about many of your own works. I have often seen you embarking on conversations with Anne Marie Rijsman-Lecluyse, Regine Walter, or Yongsoo Park, for example, and something turns out—without respect to a particular audience. And later, it seems, you find a place to share your work. Does that seem reasonable to you?

Ken: I have to agree with you that some of these efforts, especially where collaboration is involved, often begin with an unknown goal—more like playing with possibilities, and hoping that something will turn out. However, even then, I am usually concerned with the communicative and political potentials of the outcome. For example, I have misgivings even now about the success of our Bath Water musical. It did generate a lot of laughter, as we hoped. The audience could join together and laugh at the brutalizing ways we were treating each other. But there were also scholars in that audience who took offense. They felt so strongly about their political commitments that it was no joke, and our work seemed to be trivializing their efforts. In that sense we failed. On the other hand, I really love your haiku. Although I realize you wrote them for no other audience than yourself, many of them move me, and I like the way they challenge the Cartesian demand for coherence. When you survey some of the other works above, where do you see peaks and valleys?

Mary: There are some misgivings I have had over various things we have done, but for this book we have also edited out some of our worst "clinkers." I do think we agree that social scientists doing performance do not have to be high-class performers to engage in this craft. The purpose is different from what it would be if one set out only to "entertain" an audience with a highly skilled rendition. I'm thinking of a parallel in a high-school physics lab. A teacher may construct an incline plane and roll a ball down the slope to demonstrate a law of physics, and no one would reject the illustration because the ball and slide are old and scuffed. Yet, I suspect that the better a performance is artistically, the more powerful will be its effects. I think we both do worry that the baby of our arguments will be thrown out with the bathwater of our artistic renditions, if we do our performances too poorly. I know, myself, if I see someone engaging in a very amateurish performance, I cringe. Yet, actually, I am hard-pressed to recall any performance that was terrible. (Maybe some that came close.)

I also wanted to respond further on your comment about being inspired to create performances because of an invitation to present at a conference, for example. Reflecting on this, I realize that the haiku written for the Mexican conference were inspired by my assignment to comment on the experiences of the participants in this particular locale, so invitations are important to bringing forth performances. Strangely, when you first showed these to me as we were compiling this chapter, I did not recognize them as my own. They were not created with the same urgency as the high-school reunion ones, where my energies had really been stirred up. So let us say that there are many influences that come together to promote performance.

I also think our own relationship is key to our endeavors, and that we often urge each other on, give permission to be bold or outside the box in some fashion. We each enjoy the other's contributions and experiments. Our differences become a source of appreciation. (For example, I sing the melody; you sing the harmony—because you are better at it!) We can be crazy together and differently, and also, we recognize the importance of trying new paths. I do think each of us hopes our work will light fires of possibility in other creative people who may take this opening in ways we cannot imagine. We offer support to those who are making new waves, for example, Kip Jones, whom we have mentioned before, the people who present at Norman Denzin's yearly gala on qualitative methods in Champaign at the University of Illinois, and those more far-flung, from Berlin to South Africa.[1]

Ken: In the end, I also feel quite humble about our own offerings. Looking back, I think that what we have been doing is unknowingly participating in a Zeitgeist movement. Sure, we felt isolated in the early years, and then gradually we began to share affinities with an expanding group of colleagues. However, surveying events of the past two decades, I realize that performative work has been bursting out all over. Thumbing through the pages of Knowles and Cole's *Handbook of the Arts in Qualitative Research* (2008), for example, I am amazed at the amount of creative work burgeoning within the social sciences. And if I add the many new qualitative research journals that feature performative work, I see that there are now many outlets to enable the young scholar to publish and thus survive. At this point I feel "proud to be allowed to be one of the crowd."

Mary: Who knows where this will all end? I imagine a wonderful potpourri of arts and sciences—continuously transforming as it moves outward across cultures around the world. At heart, I guess I'm still a Minnesota girl, hopefully optimistic to the end.

Notes

CHAPTER 1

1. It is indeed this kind of thinking that has now spawned an array of exciting, multidisciplinary initiatives identified as *art-based research*: see, for example, Barone and Eisner (2011), Leavy (2008), and Norris (2010).

CHAPTER 2

1. See, for example, Bonney (2000), Carr (1993), Champagne (1990), and Goldberg (1979, 2007).
2. The interested reader may wish to compare Postlewait and McConachie's collection of essays on the history of performance study (1989) with Canning and Postlewait's edited work (2010). Here one can vividly witness, not only in the content but also in the dialogic and performative form of writing itself, the shift from a positivist to a constructionist orientation to performance work. See also Carlson (2003) for an account of the relationship between performance art, performance studies, and the more general cultural ethos.
3. See, for example, Holzman (1999), Newman (1994, 1996), Newman and Holzman (1996).
4. In 2004 Picart teamed with Ken to put a blended performance piece into writing: see Picart and Gergen (2004).
5. At the time of this writing, Kip is a Reader in Health Related Social Science and Leader of the Performative Social Science Group at

Bournemouth University's Centre for Qualitative Research. He also facilitates the online newsgroup Performative Social Science, and organizes an annual conference on performative social science (see www.kipworld.net).

6. Kanter's performative innovations on the topic of rebuilding community after loss (2007) represent a superb extension of this work.

7. See also his recent book, *Ethnotheatre: Research from Page to Stage* (2011).

8. These are some of the creative culprits who have enriched and sustained us over the years. There are many others: We have been wonderfully inspired by Tami Spry's autoethnographic performances (Spry 2001); Jonathan Shailor's Playback Theater approach to working with prison inmates (2010); Glenda Russell's political work in both music and video (2000); Marie Hoskins's performance collaborations with her students; the poetic adventures of Caroline Ramsey, Bob Neimeyer, and Stan Witkin; Saliha Bava's webbed dissertation and performance inquiries (https://sites.google.com/site/drbavaresearch); Margi Brown Ash's pedagogical uses of drama; and Chris Steyaert's aesthetics of organizational life, among many others. You will surely find their voices echoed in the later chapters; they are our internalized traveling companions.

CHAPTER 3

1. See, for example, Phelan and Lane (1998) and chapter 10 in Barone and Eisner (2011).

CHAPTER 9

1. For more on the effects of writing on relationships within the scholarly community see Gergen (2007).

CHAPTER 11

1. The volume resulting from the conference was edited by Steiner Kvale (1992).

2. For an appreciation of the kind of work to which I was responding, see Tyler (1987).

CHAPTER 16

1. The most extensive account of relational theory is contained in my book *Relational Being: Beyond Self and Community* (2009b).

CHAPTER 17

1. See Darnell (2011) on photography as performance.
2. For more on confluence see Gergen (2009a).
3. For more on multi-being see Gergen (2009a).

CHAPTER 26

1. See, for example, Hamera (2006), Kuppers (2003), Pineau (2002), and Warren (2003).
2. Mary wishes to thank the "girlfriends" who inspired this imaginary conversation.

CHAPTER 27

1. Many new websites also have this function of supporting and inspiring. I think here, for example, of a new website for academic video essays (http://www.audiovisualthinking.org) and our own webpage on the Taos Institute dedicated to visual resources (http://www.TaosInstitute.net).

References

Ackerman, J. M., C. C. Nocera, and J. A. Bargh. 2010. Incidental haptic sensations influence social judgments and decisions. *Science* 328: 1712–15.

Alexander, B. K. 2000. Skin flint (or the garbage man's kid): A generative autobiographical performance based on Tami Spry's Tattoo stories. *Text and Performance Quarterly* 20: 97–114.

———. 2005. Performance ethnography: The reenacting and inciting of culture. In Denzin and Lincoln 2005, 411–42. Thousand Oaks, CA: Sage.

Austin, J. L. 1962. *How To Do Things with Words*. Oxford: Blackwell.

Bakhtin, M. M. 1981. *The Dialogical Imagination*, ed. M. Holquist, trans. C. Emerson. Minneapolis: University of Minnesota Press.

Barone, T. E., and E. W. Eisner. 2011. *Arts Based Research*. Thousand Oaks, CA: Sage.

Barrows, S. B. 1987. With W. Novak. *Mayflower Madam*. Sydney: Futura Press.

Barthes, R. 1994. *Roland Barthes by Roland Barthes*, trans. Richard Howard. Berkeley, CA: University of California Press. (Orig. pub. 1977.)

Bateson, G., and M. Mead. 1942. *Balinese Character: A Photographic Analysis*. New York: New York Academy of Sciences.

Benstock, S. 1988. Authorizing the autobiography. In *The Private Self: Theory and Practice in Women's Autobiographical Writings*, ed. S. Benstock, 1–13. London: Routledge.

Boal, A. 1979. *Theater of the Oppressed*. New York: Urizen Books.

Bochner, A., and C. Ellis, eds. 2002. *Ethnographically Speaking: Autoethnography, Literature, and Aesthetics*. Walnut Creek, CA: AltaMira Press.

Bonney, J. 2000. *Extreme Exposure: An Anthology of Solo Performance Texts from the Twentieth Century*. New York: Theater Communications Group.

Brady, I. 2003. *The Time at Darwin's Reef: Poetic Exploration in Anthropology and History*. Walnut Creek, CA: AltaMira Press.

Broadhurst, S. 1999. *Liminal Acts: A Critical Overview of Contemporary Performance and Theory*. London: Cassell.

Brossard, N. 2000. A state of mind in the garden. *Journal of Lesbian Studies* 4: 35–40.

Bruss, E. 1980. Eye for I: Making and unmaking autobiography in film. In J. Olney, 296–320. Princeton, NJ: Princeton University Press.

Burke, C. G. 1978. Report from Paris: Women's writing and the women's movement. *Signs: Journal of Women in Culture and Society* 3: 843–55.

Buss, D. 1995. *The Evolution of Desire*. New York: Basic Books.

Butler, J. 1990. *Gender Trouble: Feminism and the Subversion of Identity*. New York: Routledge.

Campbell, J. 1956. *The Hero with a Thousand Faces*. New York: Bollingen.

Canning, C. M., and T. Postlewait, eds. 2010. *Representing the Past: Essays in Performance Historiography*. Iowa City: University of Iowa Press.

Carlson, M. 2003. *Performance: A Critical Introduction*. New York: Routledge.

Carr, C. 1993. *On Edge: Performance at the End of the Twentieth Century*. Hanover, NH: University Press of New England.

Champagne, L. 1990. *Out from Under: Texts by Women Performance Artists*. New York: Theater Communications Group.

Cheng, N. 1986. *Life and Death in Shanghai*. New York: Penguin.

Cho, J., and A. Trent. 2009. Validity criteria for performance-related qualitative work: Toward a reflexive, evaluative, and co-constructive framework for performance in/as qualitative inquiry. *Qualitative Inquiry* 15: 1013–41.

Chodorow, N. 1978. *The Reproduction of Mothering and the Sociology of Gender*. Berkeley, CA: University of California Press.

Chomsky, N. 1968. *Language and Mind*. Cambridge, MA: Cambridge University Press.

Clifford, J. 1986. Introduction: Partial truths. In *Writing Cultures: The Poetics and Politics of Ethnography*, eds. J. Clifford and G. Marcus, 1–26. Berkeley, CA: University of California Press.

Cole, E., and M. M. Gergen, eds. 2012. *Retiring, but not Shy: Feminist Psychologists Create Their Post-careers*. Chagrin Falls, OH: Taos Institute Publications.

Conquergood, D. 1982. Performing as a moral act: Ethical dimensions of the ethnography performance. *Literature in Performance* 5: 1–13.

———. 1989. Poetics, play, process, and power: The performative turn in anthropology. *Text and Performance Quarterly* 9: 82–88.

———. 2002. Lethal theatre: Performance, punishment, and the death penalty. *Theatre Journal* 54: 339–67.

Cooley, C. H. 1902. *Human Nature and Social Order*. New York: Charles Scribner's Sons.

Crawford, M. 1995. *Talking Difference: On Gender and Language*. Thousand Oaks, CA: Sage.

Cruz, M. R., C. Moreira, and D. Yomtoob. 2009. Transgressive borders: A performative diaspora in three movements. *Qualitative Inquiry* 15: 787–805.

Curt, B. 1994. *Textuality and Tectonics: Troubling Social and Psychological Science*. Milton Keynes, UK: Open University Press.

Daly, M. 1978. *Gyn/Ecology: The Metaethics of Radical Feminism*. Boston: Beacon Press.

Darnell, A. L. 2011. Tucked away. *Text and Performance Quarterly* 31: 401–17.

de Lauretis, T. 1984. *Alice Doesn't: Feminism, Semiotics, Cinema*. Bloomington, IN: University of Indiana Press.

de Man, P. 1979. Autobiography as de-facement. *Modern Language Notes* 94: 919–30.

Denzin, N. K. 2003. *Performance Ethnography: Critical Pedagogy and the Politics of Culture*. Thousand Oaks, CA: Sage.

Denzin, N. K., and Y. S. Lincoln. 2000. Introduction: The discipline and practice of qualitative research. In *Handbook of Qualitative Research*, eds. N. K. Denzin, and Y. S. Lincoln, 1–17. 2nd ed. Thousand Oaks, CA: Sage.

———. 2005. *Handbook of Qualitative Research*. 3rd ed. Thousand Oaks, CA: Sage.

Dikovitskaya, M. 2006. *Visual Culture: The Study of the Visual after the Cultural Turn*. Cambridge, MA: MIT Press.

Dinnerstein, D. 1976. *The Mermaid and the Minotaur: Sexual Arrangements and Human Malaise*. New York: Harper & Row.

Diversi, M. 1998. Glimpses of street life: Representing lived experience through short stories. *Qualitative Inquiry* 4: 131–37.

Douglas, M. 1966. *Purity and Danger: An Analysis of Pollution and Taboo*. New York: Routledge & Kegan Paul.

DuPlessis, R. B. 1985. *Writing beyond the Ending*. Bloomington: Indiana University Press.

Eliot, T. S. 1963. The love song of J. Alfred Prufrock. In *Collected Poems: 1909–1962*. London: Faber & Faber.

Ellis, C. 1995. *Final Negotiations: A Story of Love, Loss, and Chronic Illness*. Philadelphia: Temple University Press.

———. 2004. *The Ethnographic I: A Methodological Novel about Autoethnography*. Walnut Creek, CA: AltaMira Press.

Ellis, C., and A. Bochner, eds. 1996. *Composing Ethnography: Alternative Forms of Qualitative Writing*. Walnut Creek, CA: AltaMira Press.

Emerson, C. 1983. The outer word and inner speech: Bakhtin, Vygotsky, and the internalization of language. *Critical Inquiry* 10: 245–64.

Feynman, R. P. 1986. *"Surely you're joking, Mr. Feynman!" (Adventures of a Curious Character)*. New York: Bantam Books.

Fine, M., and S. M. Gordon. 1991. Effacing the center and the margins: Life at the intersection of psychology and feminism. *Feminism & Psychology* 1: 19–28.

Flax, J. 1983. Political philosophy and the patriarchal unconscious: A psychoanalytic perspective on epistemology and metaphysics. In *Discovering Reality*, eds. S. Harding and M. Hintikka, 245–82. Dordrecht: D. Reidel.

———. 1987. Postmodernism and gender relations in feminist theory. *Signs: Journal of Women in Culture and Society* 12: 621–43.

———. 1990. *Thinking Fragments*. Berkeley, CA: University of California Press.

———. 1993. *Disputed Subjects*. New York: Routledge.

Foucault, M. 1975. *Discipline and Punish: The Birth of the Prison*. New York: Vintage.

———. 1980. *Power/Knowledge: Selected Interviews and Other Writings, 1972–1977*. New York: Pantheon.

Fox, K. V. 1996. Silent voices: A subversive reading of child sexual abuse. In C. Ellis and A. P. Bochner, 330–56.

Freire, P. 1970. *Pedagogy of the Oppressed*. London: Continuum.

Freud, S. 1933. Femininity (Lecture 33). In *New Introductory Lectures on Psychoanalysis*, vol. 22, ed. and trans. J. Strachey, 112–35. London: Hogarth.

Geertz, C. 1983. *Local Knowledge: Further Essays in Interpretive Anthropology*. New York: Basic Books.

Gergen, K. J. 1973. Social psychology as history. *Journal of Personality and Social Psychology* 26: 308–20.

———. 1982. *Toward Transformation in Social Knowledge*. London: Sage.

———. 1991. *The Saturated Self: Dilemmas of Identity in Contemporary Life*. New York: Basic Books.

———. 1994. *Realities and Relationships: Soundings in Social Construction*. Cambridge, MA: Harvard University Press.

———. 2007. Writing as relationship in academic culture. In *Communicative Practices in Workplaces and the Professions*, eds. M. Zachry and C. Thralls, 95–102. Amityville, NY: Baywood.

———. 2009a. *An Invitation to Social Construction*. 2nd ed. London: Sage.

———. 2009b. *Relational Being: Beyond self and Community*. New York: Oxford University Press.

Gergen, K. J., and M. M. Gergen. 1983. Narrative of the self. In *Studies in Social Identity*, eds. T. Sarbin and K. Schiebe, 254–73. New York: Praeger.

———. 1988. Narrative and the self as relationship. In *Advances in Experimental Social Psychology, Vol. 21*, ed. L. Berkowitz, 17–56. San Diego: Academic Press.

———. 1991. From theory to reflexivity in research practice. In *Method and Reflexivity: Knowing as Systemic Social Construction*, ed. F. Steier, 76–95. London: Sage.

Gergen, M. M. 1988. *Feminist Thought and the Structure of Knowledge*. New York: New York University Press.

Gergen, M. M., and K. J. Gergen. 1984. Narrative structures and their social construction. In *Historical Social Psychology*, eds. K. J. Gergen and M. M. Gergen, 173–90. Hillsdale, NJ: Lawrence Erlbaum.

Getty, J. P. 1986. *As I See It: The Autobiography of J. Paul Getty*. New York: Berkely.

Gilligan, C. 1982. *In a Different Voice: Psychological Theory and Women's Development*. Cambridge, MA: Harvard University Press.

Gitlin, T. 1988. Hip-deep in post-modernism. *New York Times Book Review*, November 6.

Goffman, E. 1959. *The Presentation of Self in Everyday Life*. New York: Doubleday Anchor.

Goldberg, R. 1979. *Performance Art: From Futurism to the Present*. London: Thames and Hudson.

———. 2007. *Performa: New Visual Art Performance*. New York: Performa.

Goldstein, T., and J. Wickett. 2009. Zero tolerance: A stage adaptation of an investigative report on school safety. *Qualitative Inquiry* 15: 1552–68.

Gray, R., and C. Sinding. 2002. *Standing Ovation: Performing Social Science Research about Cancer*. Walnut Creek, CA: AltaMira Press.

Greenblat, C. S. 2004. *Alive with Alzheimer's*. Chicago: University of Chicago Press.

Hamera, J., ed. 2006. *Opening Acts: Performance in/as Communication and Cultural Studies*. Thousand Oaks, CA: Sage.

Haraway, D. 1988. Situated knowledges: The science question in feminism and the privilege of partial perspective. *Feminist Studies* 14: 575–99.

Harding, S. 1986a. The instability of the analytical categories of feminist theory. *Signs: Journal of Women in Culture and Society* 11: 645–64.

———. 1986b. *The Science Question in Feminism*. Ithaca, NY: Cornell University Press.

Heidegger, M. 1962. *Being and Time*. Trans. J. Macquarrie and E. Robinson. San Francisco: Harper. (Orig. pub. 1927.)

Heilbrun, C. 1988. *Writing a Woman's Life*. San Francisco: Woman's Press.

Holzman, L., ed. 1999. *Performing Psychology: A Postmodern Culture of the Mind*. New York: Routledge.

hooks, b. 1990. *Yearning Peace: Gender and Cultural Politics*. Boston: South End Press.

Iacocca, L. 1984. *Iacocca: An Autobiography*. With W. Novak. New York: Bantam Books.

Irigaray, L. 1985. *This Sex Which Is Not One*. Trans. C. Porter and C. Burke. Ithaca, NY: Cornell University Press.

Janet, P. 1928. *L'évolution de la mémoire et de la notion du temps*. Paris: L. Alcan.

Jelinek, E. C. 1980. *Women's Autobiography: Essays in Criticism*. Bloomington: Indiana University Press.

Jones, K. 2006. A biographical research in search of an aesthetic: The use of arts-based (re)presentations in "performative" dissemination of life stories. *Qualitative Sociological Review* 2. (open access online journal)

———. 2007. How did I get to Princess Margaret? (And how did I get her to the World Wide Web?) *Forum: Qualitative Social Research* 8 (3). (open access online journal)

Kamberelis, G., and G. Dimitriadis. 2005. *On Qualitative Inquiry: Approaches to Language and Literature Research*. New York: Teachers College Press.

Kanter, J. 2007. *Performing Loss: Rebuilding Community through Theater and Writing*. Carbondale, IL: Southern Illinois University Press.

Kauffman, L. S. 1986. *Discourses of Desire: Gender, Genre, and Epistolary Fictions*. Ithaca, NY: Cornell University Press.

Keller, E. F. 1983. Gender and science. In *Discovering Reality: Feminist Perspectives on Epistemology, Metaphysics, Methodology, and Philosophy of Science*, eds. S. Harding and M. B. Hintikka, 187–205. Dordrecht: Reidel.

Knowles, J. G., and A. L. Cole, eds. 2008. *Handbook of the Arts in Qualitative Research*. Thousand Oaks, CA: Sage.

Koch, E. 1984. *Mayor*. With W. Rauch. New York: Warner Books.

Kolodny, A. 1980. The lady's not for spurning: Kate Millett and the critics. In E. C. Jelinek, 541–62. Bloomington, IN: University of Indiana Press.

Kristeva, J. 1984. *Revolution in Poetic Language*. Trans. M. Waller. New York: Columbia University Press.

———. 1998. Toward a semiology of paragrams. In *The Tel Quel Reader*, eds. F. French and A. Lack, 25–49. New York: Routledge. (Orig. pub. 1969.)

Kuppers, P. 2003. *Disability and Contemporary Performance: Bodies on Edge*. London: Routledge.

Kvale, S., ed. 1992. *Psychology and Postmodernism*. London: Sage.

Lather, P. 1991. *Getting Smart: Feminist Research and Pedagogy within/in the Postmodern*. London: Routledge.

———. 1995. The validity of angels: Interpretive and textual strategies in researching the lives of women with HIV/AIDS. *Qualitative Inquiry* 1: 41–68.

Lather, P., and C. Smithies. 1997. *Troubling with Angels: Women Living with HIV/AIDS*. Boulder, CO: Westview.

Leavy, P. 2008. *Method Meets Art: Arts-Based Research Practice*. New York: Guilford.

———. 2009. Fractured femininities/massacred masculinities: A poetic installation. *Qualitative Inquiry* 15: 1439–47.

Lieblich, A., R. Tuval-Mashiach, and T. Zilber. 1998. *Narrative Research: Reading, Analysis, and Interpretation*. Thousand Oaks, CA: Sage.

Locke, J. 1692. *An Essay Concerning Human Understanding*. London: Buffet.

Lockford, L. 2004. *Performing Femininity: Rewriting Gender Identity*. Walnut Creek, CA: AltaMira Press.

Lorde, A. 1984. *Sister Outsider*. Berkeley, CA: Crossing Press.

Madison, D. S., and J. Hamera, eds. 2006. *The Sage Handbook of Performance Studies*. Thousand Oaks, CA: Sage.

Mason, M. G. 1980. Autobiographies of women writers. In J. Olney, 325–36.

McNiff, S. 2007. Art-based research. In *Handbook of the Arts in Qualitative Research: Perspectives, Methodologies, Examples, and Issues*, eds. G.J. Knowles and A.L. Cole. Thousand Oaks, CA: Sage.

Merleau-Ponty, M. 1964. Eye and mind. Trans. C. Dallery. In *The Primacy of Perception*, ed. J. Edie. Evanston: Northwestern University Press.

Mirzoeff, N. 2002. *The Visual Culture Reader*. 2nd ed. London: Routledge.

Mulkay, M. 1985. *The Word and the World*. London: George Allen & Unwin.

Myers, W. B., and B. K. Alexander. 2010. (Performance is) Metaphors as methodological tools in qualitative inquiry. *International Review of Qualitative Inquiry* 3: 263–67.

Navratilova, M. 1985. *Martina*. With G. Vecsey. New York: Fawcett Press.

Newman, F. 1994. *Let's Develop! A Guide to Continuous Personal Growth*. New York: Castillo International.

———. 1996. *Performance of a Lifetime: A Practical-Philosophical Guide to the Joyous Life*. New York: Castillo International.

Newman, F., and L. Holzman. 1996. *Unscientific Psychology: A Cultural-Performatory Approach to Understanding Human Life*. Westport, CT: Praeger.

Norris, J. 2010. *Playbuilding as Qualitative Research: A Participatory Arts-based Approach*. Walnut Creek, CA: Left Coast Press.

Nussbaum, F. 1988. Eighteenth century women's autobiographical commonplaces. In *The Private Self*, ed. S. Benstock, 1–13. London: Routledge.

Ochberg, R. L. 1988. Life stories and the psychosocial construction of careers. *Journal of Personality* 56: 171–202.

Olney, J., ed. 1980. *Autobiography: Essays Theoretical and Critical*. Princeton, NJ: Princeton University Press.

Owens, C. 1983. The discourse of others: Feminists and postmodernism. In *The Anti-aesthetic: Essays on Postmodern Culture*, ed. H. Foster, 57–82. Port Townsend, WA: Bay Press.

Park, H.-Y. 2009. Writing in Korean, living in the U.S.: A screenplay about a bilingual boy and his mom. *Qualitative Inquiry* 15: 1103–24.

Pearson, A. R. 2009. Scenes in the life of a woman. *Qualitative Inquiry* 15: 1448–51.

Pelias, R. 2010. Performance is an opening. *International Review of Qualitative Inquiry* 3: 173–74.

Pfohl, S. 1992. *Death at the Parasite Cafe*. New York: St Martins.

Picart, C. J., and Gergen, K. J. 2004. Dharma dancing: Ballroom dancing and the relational order. *Qualitative Inquiry* 10: 836–68.

Pineau, E. L. 2002. Critical performance pedagogy: Fleshing out the politics of liberatory education. In *Teaching Performance Studies*, eds. N. Stucky and C. Wimmer. Carbondale, IL: University of Southern Illinois Press.

Pink, S. 2009. *Doing Sensory Ethnography*. London: Sage.

Postlewait, T., and B. A. McConachie, eds. 1989. *Interpreting the Theatrical Past: Essays in the Historiography of Performance*. Iowa City: University of Iowa Press.

Rabuzzi, K. A. 1988. *Motherself: A Mythic Analysis of Motherhood*. Bloomington: Indiana University Press.

Richardson, L. 1997. *Fields of Play*. New Brunswick, NJ: Rutgers University Press.

Richardson, L., and E. A. St. Pierre. 2005. Writing: A method of inquiry. In Denzin and Lincoln, 959–78.

Rivers, J. 1986. *Enter Talking*. With R. Meryman. New York: Delacorte Press.

Ronai, C. R. 1992. The reflexive self through narrative: A night in the life of an erotic dancer/researcher. In *Investigating Subjectivity: Research of Lived Experience*, eds. C. Ellis and M. G. Flaherty, 102–24. Thousand Oaks, CA: Sage.

Rorty, R. 1981. *Philosophy and the Mirror of Nature*. Princeton, NJ: Princeton University Press.

Rosenau, E. 1992. *Postmodernism and the Social Sciences*. Princeton, NJ: Princeton University Press.

Rosenwald, G. C. 1988. A theory of multiple-case research. *Journal of Personality* 56: 239–64.

Russ, J. 1972. What can a heroine do? Or why women can't write. In *Images of Women in Fiction: Feminist Perspectives*, ed. S. Koppelman Cornillon. Bowling Green, OH: University Popular Press.

Russell, G. 2000. *Voted Out: The Psychological Consequences of Anti-gay Politics*. New York: New York University Press.

Russo, M. 1986. Female grotesque: Carnival and theory. In *Feminist Studies, Critical Studies*, ed. T. de Lauretis, 213–29. Milwaukee, WI: University of Wisconsin Press.

Ryle, G. 1984. *The Concept of Mind*. Chicago: University of Chicago Press. (Orig. pub. 1949.)

Said, E. 1983. Opponents, audiences, constituencies, community. In *The Anti-aesthetic: Essays on Postmodern Culture*, ed. H. Foster, 135–59. Port Townsend, WA: Bay Press.

Saldaña, J. 2011. *Ethnotheatre: Research from Page to Stage*. Walnut Creek, CA: Left Coast Press.

Saussure, F. 1966. *Course in General Linguistics*, eds. C. Bally and A. Sechehaye, with A. Riedlinger, trans. W. Baskin. New York: McGraw-Hill. (Orig. pub. 1916.)

Sayre, R. F. 1980. Autobiography and the making of America. In J. Olney, 43–67.

Schechner, R. 1985. Points of contact between anthropological and theatrical thought. In *Between Theater and Anthropology*. Philadelphia: University of Pennsylvania Press. (Originally presented at the Wenner-Gren international symposium on theater and ritual in 1982.)

Schneider, A., and C. Wright, eds. 2006. *Contemporary Art and Anthropology*. New York: Berg Press.

———. 2010. *Between Art and Anthropology: Contemporary Ethnographic Practice*. New York: Berg Press.

Shailor, J. 2010. *Performing New Lives: Prison Theater*. Philadelphia: Jessica Kingsley Press.

Shoffstall, G. W. 2009. Metropolis and masquerade. *Qualitative Inquiry* 15(1): 168–77.

Sills, B., and L. Linderman. 1987. *Beverly*. New York: Bantam Books.

Slife, B., and F. Richardson. 2011. The relativism of social constructionism. *Journal of Constructivist Psychology* 24: 333–39.

Smith, C. A. M. 2005. Performance text for Chicago women I love, or "Hey Girlfriend." *Qualitative Inquiry* 11: 152–56.

Smith, L. T. 1999. *Decolonizing Methodologies: Research and Indigenous Peoples*. London: Zed Books.

Smith, S. A. 1974. *Where I'm Bound: Patterns of Slavery and Freedom in Black American Autobiography*. Westport, CT: Greenwood.

———. 1987. *A Poetics of Women's Autobiography: Marginality and the Functions of Self-Representation*. Bloomington: Indiana University Press.

Snow, C. P. 1993. *The Two Cultures*. New York: Cambridge University Press.

Sprinker, M. 1980. Fictions of the self: The end of autobiography. In J. Olney, 321–42.

Spry, T. 2001. Performing autoethnography: An embodied methodological praxis. *Qualitative Inquiry* 7: 706–32.

St. Pierre, E. 1997. Circling the text: Nomadic writing practices. *Qualitative Inquiry* 3: 403–17.

Stanton, D. 1984. *The Female Autograph*. Chicago: University of Chicago Press.

Stehle, B. 1985. *Incurable Romantics*. Philadelphia: Temple University Press.

Strathern, M. 1987. Out of context: The persuasive factions of anthropology. *Current Anthropology* 28: 241–70.

Tillmann-Healy, L. M. 1996. A secret life in the culture of thinness. In Ellis and Bochner eds. 76–105.

Turner, V. 1977. *The Ritual Process: Structure and Anti-structure*. Ithaca, NY: Cornell University Press.

Tyler, S. 1986. Post-modern ethnography: From document of the occult to occult documents. In *Writing Cultures: The Poetics and Politics of Ethnography*, eds. J. Clifford and G. Marcus, 122–40. Berkeley, CA: University of California Press.

———. 1987. *The Unspeakable*. Madison, WI: University of Wisconsin Press.

Warren, J. T. 2003. *Performing Purity: Pedagogy, Whiteness, and the Reconstitution of Power*. New York: Peter Lang.

Weems, M. E. 1997. *White*. Kent, OH: Kent State University Press.

White, H. 1987. *The Content of the Form: Narrative Discourse and Historical Representation*. Baltimore: The Johns Hopkins University Press.

Whitney, D. 1995. Social constructionism and spirituality. Paper presented at Global Leadership: A Conference on Social Constructionism and Management, Taos Institute. Taos, NM.

Wittgenstein, L. 1953. *Philosophical Investigations*. London: Blackwell.

Woolf, V. 1957. *A Room of One's Own*. New York: Harcourt, Brace Jovanovich. (Orig. pub. 1929.)

———. 1958. *Granite and Rainbow*. New York: Harcourt, Brace Jovanovich.

Yeager, C., and L. Janos. 1985. *Yeager: An Autobiography*. New York: Bantam Books.

Index

About the Authors

Mary M. Gergen and Kenneth J. Gergen are among the originators of performative social science. Working both together and separately, they have been experimenting in various domains of performative social science since the 1980s. Their work has spanned literary, dramatic, and the visual arts. Both authors claim their origins in social psychology, but have long since disregarded disciplinary boundaries to generate dialogue both within the scholarly sphere and between scholars and practitioners. Mary M. Gergen is Professor Emerita, Penn State University, Brandywine, in Psychology and Women's Studies. Her primary work has been at the crossroads of feminist theory and social constructionism. Among her major writings are *Feminist Thought and the Structure of Knowledge* (1988); *Feminist Reconstructions in Psychology: Narrative, Gender, and Performance* (2001); and *Social Construction: Entering the Dialogue* (2004, with K. J. Gergen). She has performed at numerous conferences, offering dramatic monologues, often on the role of women in society. Kenneth J. Gergen is a Senior Research Professor at Swarthmore College. He has been a major contributor to social constructionist theory and to relational theory and practice. Among his major writings are *The Saturated Self: Dilemmas of Identity in Contemporary Life* (1991); *Realities and Relationships: Soundings in Social Construction* (1994); *An Invitation to Social Construction* (2009); and *Relational Being: Beyond Self and Community* (2009). His work in performative social science has focused on philosophical issues, relational processes, and meaning-making. Mary and Ken are two of the founders of the Taos Institute, a nonprofit organization bringing constructionist theory together with societal practices, including performance.